Contract Management
or Self-Operation

A Decision-Making Guide for Higher Education

Prepared by
Philip J. Goldstein, Daphne E. Kempner, and Sean C. Rush of
Coopers & Lybrand's Higher Education Consulting Group

With assistance from
Mark Bookman, J.D.,
Education and Non-Profit Consulting, Inc.

Sponsored by
The Council of Higher Education Management Associations

Published for CHEMA by APPA:
The Association of Higher Education Facilities Officers
1446 Duke Street
Alexandria, Virginia 22314-3492

Walter A. Schaw: Project Steering Committee Coordinator
Steve Glazner: Publication Coordinator

International Standard Book Number: 0-913359-73-4

Printed in the United States of America.

Printed on acid-free paper.

Table of Contents

Preface

The 1990s have been and will continue to be a decade of constraint for higher education. Declining enrollments, decreased funding for research, state budget cuts, and increasing pressure to limit tuition growth have resulted in diminished availability of traditional revenue sources. Many schools are fundamentally reassessing the ways in which they do business as well as which businesses they should be in. While this self-evaluation must eventually include the institution's educational, research, and public service missions, much attention has already been focused on the auxiliary enterprises as schools seek opportunities to decrease expenditures, increase revenue, or both.

Increasingly, privatization (also referred to as contract management or outsourcing) is being considered as a tool in this battle to do more with less. Privatization in higher education refers to the decision to contract with an external organization to provide (or manage the provision of) a traditional campus function or service. While contract management has been used to operate the campus bookstore or dining service for years, it has more recently become an operating alternative for a diverse set of campus functions including facilities, administrative computing, security, and child care. In fact, virtually any campus function or service, including instruction, is theoretically subject to privatization.

Is privatization good for higher education? You will not receive many noncommittal answers to this question. The issue of contract management is emotionally charged with large numbers of fervent supporters and detractors. Supporters see it as a way to shed headaches, stabilize or increase income, control or lessen expenses, and to concentrate on the core mission of education by leaving the provision of services to the external companies who are best equipped to provide them. Detractors see it as a loss of institutional control, less responsive service, higher costs to students, displaced employees, an erosion of an institution's identity, lack of understanding or support for the mission of the institution, and at best a short-term gain that will be more than offset by long-term losses. Who is right?

This guide does not seek to offer an answer to this question. In fact, the question is best answered on a case-by-case, campus-by-campus, and function-by-function basis. Instead, we offer an objective framework for deciding for yourself how best to operate any function on your campus. Our emphasis is on the questions, stakeholders, and analysis that go into determining whether self-operation, contract management, or some combination of the two will offer the best opportunities for meeting the goals and objectives you have set out for a functional area.

The guide is organized into four chapters. Chapter I briefly outlines the evolution of contract management in higher education and presents six real-life scenarios in which institutions faced the contract management/self-operation decision. Chapter II presents an approach that can be utilized by managers of any functional area as well as an institution's chief business officer to identify, assess, and interpret the many issues that need to be considered prior to choosing the right management approach for an institution.

The third chapter demonstrates how the general approach outlined in Chapter II can be applied to six specific functional areas:

- Facilities

- Bookstore

- Dining services

- Administrative computing

- Child care

- Security.

Only the provision of a service can be contracted for, not the responsibility for it. In the eyes of the customer, the ultimate accountability will always rest with the institution.

This mix of functions includes areas that have traditionally utilized contract management: the bookstore and dining services; an area that has been traditionally self-operated: administrative computing; two functions that employ a combination of self-operation and contract management: facilities and security; and an emerging campus service: child care — for which many campus administrators are facing the contract management/self-operation question for the first time. Chapter IV revisits the six case vignettes of the first chapter and reveals for each case the operating model that was ultimately selected and why.

The reader is urged to review the guide in its entirety prior to focusing in depth on the individual functional areas contained in Chapter III. Concepts and questions included in the discussions of the individual functional areas often have a more general application as well. In order to prevent the guide from becoming repetitive, these concepts have been introduced in the discussion of the functions to which they are most applicable. For instance, a legal or financial issue raised in the discussion of the bookstore might also be applicable to a discussion of child care.

The research for this guide was conducted primarily through interviews and surveys of institutions that have recently considered a change in their approach to managing one or more of the functional areas that the guide focuses on. In addition, vendors who provide contract management services to higher education were contacted to gain their insights into the decision process. Finally, we reviewed a sampling of the literature that has previously been written on this topic.

Some of the literature suggests that responsibility for a service or function can be shifted by contracting. Such conclusions are confusing the *performance* of a function with the *responsibility* for the function. A prominent governor has said that government's responsibility is not to provide services to its citizens, but rather to see that needed services are provided. The same can be said of a college or university. Managers need the flexibility to employ whatever operational approach best offers cost-efficient, high quality service in a manner that is consistent with the institution's strategy, mission, and culture. At the same time, managers who consider contract management must do so with the realization that only the provision of a service can be contracted for, not the responsibility for it. In the eyes of the customer, the ultimate accountability will always rest with the institution.

Chapter I.
The Origins of Contract Management

The college or university of today is expected to provide far more to its students than an education. Schools, both large and small, create entire communities for their students, faculty, and staff offering everything from housing to mail services. As the infrastructure of institutions has grown, so too have support organizations such as computing centers, campus police forces, and facilities management organizations. In fact, it is not uncommon for the campus of today to find itself simultaneously operating a large police force, several dining halls and catering businesses, a multimillion dollar retail operation, a child care center, and other business enterprises in support of its educational mission.

The contract management/ self-operation decision provides an opportunity to continuously assess the performance of an operation and to proactively select the model best suited for the institution.

Prior to World War II, institutions had little or no choice other than to operate these services themselves. With the growth of enrollments following the war, colleges and universities found themselves operating dining services and bookstores that were often larger in size and complexity than those in the private sector. As these operations grew, they became attractive potential clients to private corporations. Vendors began to offer to run an institution's bookstore or dining service in exchange for a flat fee or a percentage of operating revenue. These companies offered the promise of proven systems and professional management that would reduce expenditures while increasing revenues and customer service.

Today, contract management has become an option for providing a wide range of campus services including administrative computing, facilities management, child care, legal services, investment management, campus security, and many others. In fact, virtually any service can theoretically be provided through contract management. It is conceivable that in the near future, institutions will have the option of using a contractor to run their bursars office, fundraising operation, treasury function, and other non-academic services. This trend reflects the growing need for college and university management to have the flexibility to employ a wide range of options to respond to the increasing complexity of their operations and the ever decreasing level of available resources. The availability of a variety of models of operation, including contract management, self-operation, or a hybrid approach, presents management with the opportunity to continuously assess the performance of their own operations and to proactively select the models that are best suited to their institutions.

Institutions embark on the contract management/self-operation decision for any number of reasons. Traditionally, it has been the emergence of an operational or financial crisis such as large operating losses, internal theft or management fraud, or the unexpected departure of the functional area's manager that has provided the impetus for changing management approach. More recently, institutions have sought to change their management approach as a way to raise the level and quality of customer service or improve financial performance or as the result of a strategic decision to refocus the institution's management resources on those areas that are directly related to institutional mission.

The remainder of this chapter presents a series of actual case vignettes that are representative of the range of issues that give rise to the contract management decision. For each case, the outcome of the decision process is presented in Chapter IV.

Vignette #1

The vice president for facilities of a large urban university has just completed a self-assessment of his department's operations. He believes that the custodial portion of the operation is over-staffed in comparison to other institutions and industry benchmarks and that the institution is not receiving a level of service that is commensurate with the investment it is making in its custodial operations. The vice president decides to explore his options for contracting for the provision of custodial services. After seeking the input of customers, legal and union advisors, and current facilities management, a detailed set of specifications is developed that includes a building-by-building description of the level and frequency of custodial services that the university expects a vendor to provide. Bids are received from several vendors and vendor references are checked. In a presentation to the senior vice president and president, the vice president for facilities recommends that the institution accept a bid from a vendor who is offering to provide the required level and quality of services at an annual savings of $1.5 million to the institution.

Vignette # 2

The treasurer of a small suburban liberal arts college has received a proposal from the school's dining services vendor to renew its contract. The proposal offers the college significantly less revenue than the institution's current contract. This is consistent with a historical pattern that has developed at the school. A vendor offers the college a favorable initial contract that it is then unable to maintain in subsequent contracts. As a result, the college has had a series of vendors manage its dining services, with no vendor remaining beyond the initial contract. In addition, the college's students are unhappy with the quality and variety of the food and want a menu that is more tailored to the college's large contingent of vegetarians.

Vignette # 3

A small suburban liberal arts college has historically contracted with a vendor to manage its campus bookstore. The current vendor's contract has just expired and although that vendor has performed satisfactorily, many members of the college's faculty and staff feel that the institution could do a better job by self-operating. The administration is concerned that the school will not be able to operate the store as cost-effectively as the vendor has. While they agree that self-operation would be more in keeping with the school's culture, they want a detailed understanding of the likely costs associated with self-operation before they agree to a change.

Vignette # 4

A new senior management team has been put in place at a large urban university. As one of the outcomes of its assessment of the university's current financial and operational condition, the decision is made to upgrade the institution's information systems. Senior management is not confident that the current administrative computing leadership has the capabilities to perform a complicated multi-year systems implementation. Further, it is their assessment that the university has not been receiving an acceptable level of return on its investment in technology.

Vignette # 5

The long-time director of physical plant for a small liberal arts college has suffered a heart attack that causes him to choose early retirement. The current assistant director is relatively inexperienced and is not prepared to take on the director's job. The college's treasurer is faced with the choice of conducting a search for a new director or contracting with a vendor to manage the department. Further compounding the decision is a recent report from a facilities consulting firm that concluded that the facilities department was not operating efficiently and needed to upgrade and modernize its procedures and the level of knowledge of its workforce. The college has recently completed construction of a new science center and the board of trustees is not confident that the current facilities department has the skills to maintain its more complex systems. Historically, the facilities department has required a disproportionate amount of the treasurer's time and she wants the new management team to be able to run the department without as much day-to-day direction from her.

★★★★★

In each of these cases, the institution's business officer, often in consultation with the functional area manager, is facing a strategic choice as to how to best provide a service to the campus community. The outcome of each decision will have an impact on a broad array of factors including the institution's mission and strategy, personnel, financial performance, and customer satisfaction. To be successful, each decision maker needs to look beyond issues of financial performance and management convenience in choosing among the available alternatives. While each of the scenarios presented above is unique, there is a *core set of issues* that needs to be evaluated and a common approach that can be applied to *any such* decision.

Chapter II.
Conceptual Decision Process

Regardless of the specific function, service, or activity, there is a core set of issues and questions that management needs to consider in every contract management and/or self-operation decision. These core "decision factors" can be grouped into six categories:

- *Financial* — the direct and indirect cost to the institution of providing the service through each of the operational/management options available to them.

- *Human Resources* — the effect on employees both within and outside the functional area being considered, including the impact on employee compensation, staffing levels, performance evaluation, and compliance with AA/EEO policies.

- *Mission and Culture* — the impact on the institution's mission and culture and the implications of choosing an alternative that is not consistent with the institution's historical mission and culture.

- *Management Control and Efficiency* — the likely impact that each option will have on the institution's ability to control the overall direction and operational priorities of the functional area and the implications of choosing a management philosophy that features decreased or increased control. Does the institution have the necessary management infrastructure (people, systems, facilities) in place to provide a particular service? Can these capabilities be acquired cost-effectively?

- *Service Quality* — the effect each option will have on meeting the needs of its primary customers (students, faculty, and staff).

- *Legal and Ethical Considerations* — the level of risk and potential for liability posed by each option, potential conflicts of interest, tax ramifications, and the potential pitfalls and power of the contract.

The relative importance that each of these decision factors has in selecting an operating model will vary from institution to institution and between functional areas. For instance, legal considerations may weigh more heavily in a decision to operate a child care center than it would for dining services, while human resource considerations may play a more important role in selecting the operating method for a rural campus than an urban one.

While the circumstances faced by each campus are unique, the actual decision process is the same. To be successful, campus decision makers need to employ a structured methodology that enables them to consider a wide range of issues and to arrive at a decision that is in the best interest of the institution and that can withstand the close scrutiny of the many members of the campus community who are likely to have strong opinions on this topic. This is true regardless of the size of the institution. The decision factors that must be weighed by a large university are the same ones that are faced by a small college. Therefore, even if an institution does not have the resources to exactly follow the committee driven approach presented in this guide, the issues and questions that are raised by the decision process are still applicable.

While no approach can be foolproof, we believe that the process described in the remainder of this chapter provides a useful vehicle for:

- Assessing the strengths and weaknesses of your current operation

- Building consensus through the decision process

- Identifying the operating alternatives available to the institution

- Choosing an operating approach that maximizes benefits and minimizes disruptions.

The major components or phases of the decision process are as follows:

1. ***Identify Key Participants***

2. ***Develop Analytical Framework***

3. ***Assess the Current Environment***

4. ***Identify Customer Requirements***

5. ***Develop Operating Design***

6. ***Identify Operating Alternatives***

7. ***Review Legal, Ethical, and Community Considerations***

8. ***Compare and Contrast Proposed Alternatives***

9. ***Select Preferred Alternative***

10. ***Establish Continuous Assessment/Improvement Process***

The remainder of this chapter describes the goals and objectives of each phase, identifies the component worksteps, and weaves the phases together into a decision framework. Figure 1 on the facing page presents an overview of the structured decision process.

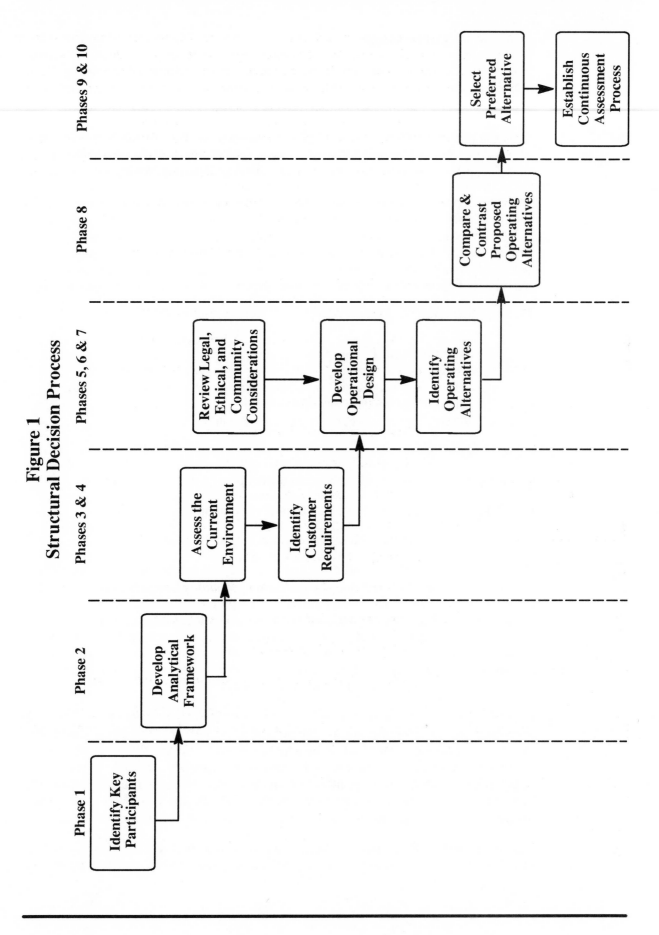

Figure 1
Structural Decision Process

Phase 1 – Identify Key Participants

Objective: To assemble a multidisciplinary team of individuals from around the institution who will perform the analysis of the alternative operating models, participate in the selection of the preferred alternative, and lead the effort to build a consensus for the chosen alternative.

While the decision to self-operate or contract will most often rest with a single or small group of decision makers (frequently the chief financial officer, vice president for auxiliary services, president, board of trustees), the decision maker(s) should seek the input of a variety of individuals from both within and outside the campus community. The use of a committee structure as opposed to a sole decision maker will encourage a more informed decision that has a broad base of support around the campus. The majority of the institutions that we spoke with or surveyed reported that they utilized a committee to evaluate the alternatives available to them for operating their functional areas. This is an important first step in building consensus for the ultimate solution which will provide for a smoother transition to the new management approach, regardless of whether it is self-operation, contract management, or a hybrid solution.

The individual activities that comprise Phase 1 are described below.

1.1 Identify Functional Participants

In order to analyze the diverse set of issues that make up each of the "decision factors" previously identified, the decision maker will require the input of individuals with a number of different skill sets. The committee or project team should include:

- A financial analyst

- An individual knowledgeable about the institution's human resource policies

- An advisor familiar with the functional area's operation

- A legal advisor familiar with issues of contracting and liability.

The challenge is to select a team that will accurately and objectively assess each alternative.

There are a variety of opinions as to whether to include the functional area manager in the decision-making process. Many feel that the manager would be unable to provide objective judgments because he or she may perceive that the proposal to change management approaches is a result of dissatisfaction with his or her ability and if adopted will force him or her out of a job. (It should be noted that in cases of changing from self-operation to contract management, the present manager in some cases is retained.) Others argue that only the present manager can truly understand the complexities of operating the particular function on the campus and, as a result, is vital to the decision process.

The challenge facing the decision maker is to select a group of individuals who will provide an accurate and objective assessment of the capabilities of the current operation as well as of each proposed alternative. Whether or not your functional area manager can play this role is up to you to determine. Other alternatives that have been employed successfully by institutions include hiring an outside consultant either from an independent firm or from another institution. Here again, the key consideration is objectivity. You should be careful to select an individual who has no preconceived bias for or against either self-operation or contract management.

Other participants on the project team should include an individual who can help perform the analysis of the relative costs associated with each proposed alternative. Also included should be an individual who can provide insight into the many human resource-related questions that will evolve during discussions with vendors. This should be an individual who can also advise the decision maker on how to involve the present employees of the functional area in the decision process and, in the case of a change in management teams, how to best help employees through that transition. In addition, this individual can assist the project team in understanding issues such as affirmative action, equal employment opportunity, and employee performance evaluation. In most cases, this individual will be a representative of the institution's personnel or human resource department. In the case of functional areas that involve the presence of a unionized workforce, the institution's chief labor negotiator should be involved. Finally, the decision maker will need the input of a lawyer familiar with contracting for services in higher education, including issues of unfair competition, unrelated business income tax, and legal liability.

1.2 Identify Constituent Representatives

It is important that the committee contain at least one representative of each of the major internal constituent groups of the functional area. In most cases, a functional area's constituents will comprise its present and planned customers. So, in the case of dining services, the constituent representatives should be made up of students, faculty, and staff, but might also need to include catering and conference planning staff. In selecting the constituent representatives, the goal is to involve in the decision process representatives of the groups that will later judge the success or failure of the ultimate operating approach that is selected. The greater the extent to which these groups can be involved in the decision process, the greater will be their degree of support for the new management approach.

Equally important as their political role, the constituent representatives should be given the lead responsibility for outlining the needs of the functional area's customers. These individuals will also be responsible for providing customer input into the evaluation of the strengths and weaknesses of the current operation and should assist in the development or refinement of the functional area's mission statement. The better these representatives understand the challenges faced by the institution in providing a particular service or function, the better they will be able to "sell" this idea to the greater campus community.

1.3 Kick-off Meeting

The purpose of the kick-off meeting is to ensure that everyone understands the goals and objectives of the decision process and knows what their roles and responsibilities in that process are. It is very important to use the kick-off meeting as a forum in which all participants can express any pre-existing concerns or biases they have about contract management/self-operation in general or about its specific impact on the campus. The sooner these concerns are expressed, the sooner they can be researched and resolved in an objective, factual manner. Left unaddressed, these concerns can potentially reduce the decision process to an emotional and reactive activity that does not let the facts fuel the ultimate decision.

The kick-off meeting also offers an opportunity for the decision maker to communicate his or her expectations to the group. It is useful to explain to each member that the committee is a working group with each member playing a lead role in assessing one or more of the decision factors. In fact, the entire decision process should be presented to the group at this time, highlighting how the various components of the analysis will be brought together. Figure 2 on the following page may be useful in facilitating such a discussion. Finally, this initial meeting provides an opportunity to handle any administrative issues such as meeting dates, administrative support, and expected timeline.

Figure 2
Conceptual Decision Process

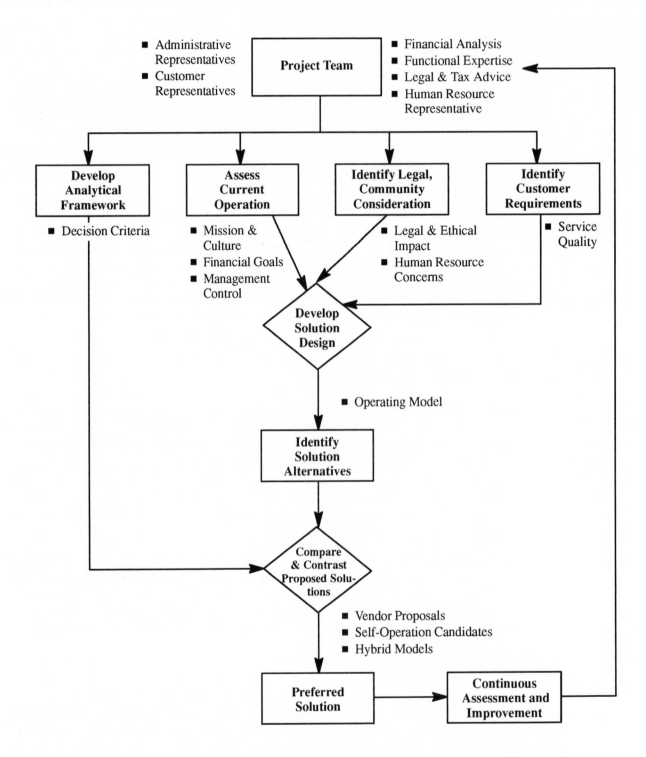

Phase 2 – Develop Analytical Framework

Objective: To identify the framework within which each solution alternative will be assessed in order to provide a structure for evaluating each option and to ensure that the ultimate decision will withstand close scrutiny.

It is unlikely that in the course of the decision process a single solution will be discovered that meets every one of the institution's requirements for the functional area. The reality is that each option that the committee considers will be strong in some areas, but weak in others. What the decision process is really about then is the identification and assessment of the trade-offs between each alternative. In the end, the solution that is selected should be the one whose strengths most closely mirror the priorities of the institution. Each institution must decide what the optimum balance is between such diverse criteria as management control or convenience, financial performance, cost of the service to customers, quality, customer satisfaction, and investment in infrastructure, to name a few.

By establishing a set of uniform criteria against which each solution will be assessed, the institution will be able to concretely determine which alternative best meets its needs. By establishing and adopting these criteria in conjunction with the committee, the decision maker can ensure that each alternative will be evaluated in terms of the factors that are most important to each of the major campus constituencies and to the institution as a whole. Further, by rank ordering the criteria, the decision maker can ensure that the priorities of the institution are reflected in the operating alternative that is selected.

The remainder of this section describes the activities that comprise Phase 2.

By establishing a set of uniform criteria, the institution will be able to concretely determine which alternative best meets its needs.

2.1 Develop Decision Criteria

The decision criteria should be developed jointly with the project committee. Constituent representatives may want to broaden the discussion by consulting with members of the groups they are representing. This can be accomplished by conducting focus groups or through one-on-one interviews with a representative sample of the major constituent groups. In addition, professional and trade associations can also be sources for criteria. It is important that the decision process not proceed beyond this step until the project team agrees that the evaluation criteria adequately reflect the major factors on which they believe the decision to contract or self-operate should be based.

At the same time, it is the responsibility of the decision maker to not let the project get bogged down at this stage. He or she must make it clear to the committee that the criteria are not intended to take the place of detailed customer requirements nor are they intended to be detailed quantitative performance measures or performance specifications. A list of questions that can be used to help build the evaluation criteria is included in Appendix B.

2.2 Prioritize Decision Criteria

After the committee has agreed on the criteria by which each alternative will be assessed, it is necessary to rank order the criteria. The rankings need to be consistent with the institution's overall strategy and direction and its expectations for the functional area's performance. At this stage in the process, it will be necessary to involve senior management to define and explain to the committee the institution's needs and expectations for the management and operation of the functional area. In many cases, these expectations may have already been outlined in the functional area's mission statement. If this is the case, the committee in conjunction with senior management should reevaluate the mission statement and revise it as necessary to reflect the changing priorities of the institution.

After the committee has an understanding of institutional priorities and strategy as they pertain to the functional area under consideration, the group should rank the criteria in order of importance. Several methods can be employed to accomplish this. The criteria can be ranked in order of descending importance, criteria can be grouped into broad categories — critical, very important, important — or a weighting factor can be attached to each criteria that quantitatively expresses its importance vis à vis the other criteria.

The criteria that the committee adopts at the outcome of this phase will provide a broad framework for the analytical work that will be undertaken in Phases 3 and 4. The criteria are not intended to take the place of a detailed definition of operational and customer requirements. In fact, after Phase 5 of the process is completed the prioritized criteria should be revised as necessary to reflect the information gathered in the preceding phases.

Phase 3 – Assess the Current Environment

Objective: To perform an objective assessment of the strengths and weaknesses of the current functional area and relevant institutional attributes, including the strength of its management and operating systems, the condition of its infrastructure, and the degree to which it is meeting the needs of the institution and its customers.

The majority of the institutions that were contacted as part of the research for preparing this guide cited an objective assessment of the current functional area as a vital first step in the decision process. It was their opinion that without the knowledge gained through such an evaluation, the institution would be selecting a management approach without an understanding of what it wants to achieve by changing operating models. Only by understanding what the current operation does well and what it does poorly, and more importantly, why it performs the way it does, will the institution be able to decide which operating alternative offers the best chance of replicating the strengths of the current organization while minimizing its weaknesses. Further, unless the institution understands the impediments to success (inadequate facilities, inefficient business process, lack of management information, etc.) that the current operation faces and devises a way to remove those hurdles, it is unlikely that the a new operating approach will be able to achieve significantly better results than the existing one.

The current operation should be assessed in terms of its:
- *Financial Performance*
- *Policies & Procedures*
- *Strength of Personnel*
- *Customer Satisfaction*

It is at this point in the decision process that the decision maker must determine if the current management team can perform an objective assessment of the functional area's operations. Clearly, in cases where the function is currently being managed by a contractor, it would be inappropriate for the vendor's management team to perform the evaluation. However, it should be used as a source of information about the operation. As mentioned in the discussion of Phase 1, other options include having an independent consultant or consulting firm or an experienced manager from another institution perform a management and/or financial audit of the functional area. The important thing is to choose an individual or individuals who offer the best combination of objectivity, knowledge about the functional area, knowledge about the institution and proven experience in performing an assessment of this kind.

The individual activities that comprise Phase 3 are described next.

3.1 Benchmark Current Operations

The functional area's current operations should be assessed in terms of the following categories:

- Financial Performance

- Policies and Procedures

- Strength of Personnel

- Customer Satisfaction.

It is likely that at many institutions the functional area's performance in one or more of these categories will be known prior to beginning the decision process. However, this is an important opportunity to develop as complete a picture of all of the strengths and weaknesses of the functional area as possible. This is especially true for institutions that have historically contracted with a vendor to provide the service or function. For these institutions, this may provide the first opportunity to completely assess the vendor's performance since the contract was awarded.

In assessing the current operation, it is important to include the following:

Financial — In assessing the functional area's financial performance, it is important to consider both the revenue produced (where appropriate) and the cost to provide the service. The financial performance should be looked at both historically (last five years) as well as prospectively (next 3–5 years). It is important when assessing the cost of providing the service to consider:

- What is the growth in employee compensation, including benefits, likely to be?

- What is the level of investment that the functional area will require from the institution in order to maintain or enhance its operations?

- What is the cost of providing central administrative support to the function (include accounting, human resource, payroll, facilities maintenance, etc.)?

- What is the cost of senior management time that is spent overseeing the function's operations?

- How does the activity compare to peer group financial results?

- Does the activity fund or subsidize units or activities other than through its rental payments or disbursement of year-end profits?

- For contract managed functions — How much revenue has the institution forgone by utilizing a contractor? Conversely, what levels and types of costs has the institution not had to bear as the result of contract management?

Policies & Procedures — In assessing this aspect of the functional area's operation, the institution should seek answers to questions including:

- Are there policies which address management issues?

- Do the functional area's policies and programs support the institutional mission?

- Do the current policies strike an optimum balance between efficiency and control?

- Do current procedures make the best use of an employee's time and abilities?

- Do the functional area's policies place the appropriate level of emphasis on customer service?

- Do the functional area's policies and procedures ensure compliance with applicable laws and codes?

- Does the functional area operate in a way that is consistent with industry standards?

Strength of Staff — The institution should consider contracting with an independent party (for instance, a comparable manager at a peer institution) to assess the ability of the current staff. Questions to consider during this phase of the assessment include:

- Is current management responsive, efficient, and effective?

- Has management achieved the results it said it would?

- Is management providing leadership for employees?

- What level of staff and/or management turnover has the institution experienced in the functional area? What impact has this had on operations?

- Does current management promote innovation and cooperation?

- Do employees receive sufficient levels of training?

- Does management work within the fiscal boundaries provided them?

Customer Satisfaction — This part of the assessment should be performed in conjunction with Phase 4 of the decision process and will be discussed in detail in that section of the guide.

3.2 Assess the Infrastructure

The condition of the functional area's infrastructure plays a large role in determining its likelihood for current and future success. A functional area's infrastructure comprises the building or buildings that house it, its equipment and fixtures, and its information systems. As in the operations assessment performed in the prior activity, the institution should consider calling on an individual or group of individuals knowledgeable about the functional area's operations to assess the adequacy of the infrastructure. Specifically, their review should focus on:

- Are the functional area's plant and equipment hindering its ability to provide high-quality service, minimize costs, and maximize revenue?

- Are the annual costs for upkeep of the infrastructure in line with the functional area's peers and are they assessed in the same manner?

- Is the functional area's infrastructure comparable in age, functions, and features to that of its peers?

- What is the likely level of investment required to modernize the infrastructure?

- Does the functional area have the necessary information systems to operate efficiently?

- Do the systems interact effectively with the school's administrative information systems?

The information gained through this activity will be used to estimate the comparative level of effort and cost to the institution that would be required to address any deficiencies in its infrastructure under self-operation or contract management.

3.3 Review and Update Functional Area Mission Statement

Many of the campus administrators who were contacted during the course of this study cited the presence of a clear and up-to-date mission statement as a primary contributor to the ultimate success of a functional area manager. An effective mission statement should set out the institution's expectations for the functional area's performance and its role in achieving the larger institution's strategy. Issues to be addressed include the balance between the costs of the service and its expected financial contribution to the institution, the level and nature of operating support that the institution expects to provide to the functional area, and a statement of who the functional area's primary and secondary customers are. If a mission statement for the functional area already exists, it should be reviewed by the project team to determine whether it is still valid given the changing environment that is confronting most educational institutions today.

3.4 Identify Areas of Strength, Weakness, and Opportunity

Using the information gathered during the previous three activities, the project team should direct its functional advisor to develop a written report that presents the strengths and weaknesses of the present operation. This document is not intended to be a report card on the current functional area management team. Instead, it is to be used in conjunction with the customer requirements developed in the next phase to identify:

- The features of the current operation that the institution wants to replicate in the new management approach

- The opportunities for improving the functional area's operations that should be achieved in the future

- Any impediments to the functional area's success that need to be eliminated either by the institution or the functional area management.

Phase 4 – Identify Customer Requirements

Objective: To understand who the functional area's customers are and what their expectations are for the breadth, depth, and quality of services to be provided.

Equal in importance to a functional area's financial and operational performance in determining its success is its ability to satisfy the needs of its customers. Before an institution can select the operating approach that will best serve its customers, it needs to have a detailed understanding of the types of services that the functional area should be providing as well as the level of customer satisfaction with the services that are currently provided. The distinction between satisfaction and expectations is an important one. Even though a functional area is offering a world-class level of service, it will not be successful unless it is offering the services that its customers desire or need. In addition, a function might be incurring higher operating expenses in an attempt to achieve a level of service quality that is beyond its customers' expectations. Therefore, in order to describe the right set of customer requirements to potential operators of a functional area, it is necessary to understand who the area's customers are, what their level of satisfaction is, and what their expectations are.

4.1 Identify Customer Groups/Constituencies

The project team needs to identify the primary and secondary customers of the functional area as the first step in executing this phase. Customer groups can be identified by utilizing existing customer studies, industry publications, and open discussions among the project team. In identifying the customer groups, it is important to look beyond the present customers of the function to identify potential or secondary customers as well. This may include prospective students, faculty recruits, conference attendees, visiting faculty and staff, members of the local community or members of the extended campus community. In understanding its customer base, the institution must also take into account changing trends in its composition. For instance, if the student population is shifting from traditional residential students to nontraditional commuter students, the services the campus needs to provide will also need to change.

4.2 Conduct Customer Surveys and Focus Groups, As Needed

The project team should rely heavily on its constituent representatives to conduct this portion of the analysis. These individuals were selected because of their first-hand knowledge of the issues and concerns facing their respective constituent groups. Customer information can be gathered through surveys and focus groups as well as through individual interviews with key members of a constituent groups. Surveys are useful for taking a look at a broad cross-section of a population group on a variety of issues, while focus groups are better utilized for delving in depth into one or two issues. Therefore, it is often most beneficial to use focus groups to follow up on the handful of key issues that were identified in the surveys. With large institutions or functional areas with many different constituent groups, or if the institution faces an operational decision with very strong political ramifications, the institution may want to consider having an independent party design and administer the surveys and focus groups. This will provide for more credible results and a greater sense of assurance that the survey methodology that was employed was statistically sound. It may be possible on some campuses to utilize a faculty member to play this role. However, this is only recommended in cases where the faculty is not a primary stakeholder in the outcome of the decision process.

4.3 Document Customer Requirements

The information gathered during open discussions, interviews, surveys, and focus groups should be summarized into a statement of customer requirements. This document should identify the major customer groups of the functional area and should describe the types and level of service that each expects the functional area to provide. In addition, the document should report those things that the customers believe the functional area does best and those things that they would like to see done differently. The requirements presented in the document should be prioritized to reflect the relative importance of major and minor customer groups. While it is important that the institution select an operating approach that meets as many customer needs as possible, it will not be practical to meet them all. It is likely that a number of customer requirements may prove too costly to provide or that a secondary customer group may voice a requirement that is in conflict with one expressed by the majority of customers. Clearly, in these cases it is most important to design an operating model that meets the requirements that will provide the greatest benefit to the greatest number of customers.

Taken with the statement of strengths, opportunities, and weaknesses prepared in the previous phase, the customer requirements will form the basis for an operational design for the functional area. The operational design, described in greater detail in Phase 5 of the decision process, will be used by vendors as well as in-house managers to inform their descriptions of how they would operate the function to meet the needs of the campus. The majority of the institutions surveyed and interviewed as part of this study identified the ability of the institution to articulate a detailed description of its vision for how the functional area should operate as being critical to the decision process.

Phase 5 – Develop Operational Design

Objective: To issue a statement of requirements that defines the institution's expectations and needs for the operation of the functional area that can be used by vendors as well as internal management to prepare their proposals for operating the function.

In this phase, all of the research and self-evaluation performed in the prior phases will be brought together into a comprehensive vision for the functional area's operation. The document should include the area mission, short- and long-term goals, operational requirements, required investments in plant and equipment, and performance standards. The operational design will be used as a request for proposal to guide vendors in preparing their proposals for operating the function. Internal management would also use the operational design to build its case for how self-operation could meet the objectives and requirements described in the vision. The more specific the institution can be in describing the type of operation it is seeking, the greater the opportunity will be for forging an effective working relationship with the functional area's management.

5.1 Prepare Draft Design

A member or members of the project team should be given the responsibility for preparing a draft operational design. The major components of the design should include:

- Functional Area Mission

- Short- and Long-Term Financial and Operational Goals

- Statement of Requirements for Scope and Quality of Services

- Required Improvements to Infrastructure

- Human Resource Policy

- Description of Evaluation Criteria for Selecting Management Team.

Preparation of the operational design should be based almost completely on the work performed in the prior phases and should require little if any additional research. While the level of detail that can be incorporated into this document will vary from case to case, the project team should try to be as specific as possible regarding the major policy and operational issues that face the institution.

At this point in the decision process, the project team needs to define and articulate its human resource requirements. Included in this discussion should be employee compensation levels, staff retention, and employee performance evaluation. Key questions that the project team needs to answer include:

For contract management

- Should the vendor be required to retain the functional area's current staff? If so, for how long? If not, how else might current staff be redeployed?

- Will the vendor be required to maintain the staff's current compensation and benefit levels?

- Who will have the power to dismiss an employee of the functional area?

- If not all current staff are retained, will retraining or outplacement assistance be provided by the vendor?

For self-operation:

- What level of compensation is the institution prepared to offer to attract and retain a quality manager and staff?

- (If moving from contract management) What proportion of the vendor's staff can be recruited to work for the institution?

- Does the institution have any moral or ethical responsibility to redeploy staff that are neither hired by the institution or retained by the vendor?

Clearly, these are difficult questions, the answers to which will vary from institution to institution. Many of the institutions we spoke with who chose to contract management reported that more than half of the contract negotiations were devoted to human resource questions.

5.2 Review Draft with Project Team

The draft operational design should be reviewed by the project team to insure that it accurately presents the team's vision for the functional area's operation. Again, the document should be reviewed by someone with operational experience in the functional area to make sure that the institution is describing its requirements in a way that will be familiar to respondents. The drafting of the operational design provides another opportunity for promoting a sense of ownership in the decision process for key constituent groups. Therefore, the project team may want to consider reviewing the draft with representatives of those groups. These reviewers must be carefully selected to prevent the process from bogging down into a discussion of the operational details instead of an affirmation of the objectives and priorities set forth in the vision.

5.3 Prepare Final Design Document

The document should be revised as necessary to reflect the input of the reviewers. The final document will be utilized in preparing request for proposals, developing performance standards and contractual requirements, and to measure the progress of the new operating team.

Phase 6 – Identify Operating Alternatives

Objective: To identify the range of operating alternatives available to the institution including self-operation, contract management, or a hybrid solution and to identify specific vendors that provide contract services in the functional area.

Developing a hybrid solution can offer an opportunity to combine the best attributes of contract management and self-operation.

Several institutions that were contacted as part of this study are operating their functional areas in creative ways that go beyond the apparent choices of contract management or self-operation. Developing a hybrid solution can offer an institution the opportunity to combine the best attributes of contract management and self–operation. For instance, one institution we spoke with is operating its dining services through a hybrid model that has the vendor performing the operational tasks of preparing meals, purchasing supplies, and managing staff, while the institution retains control over setting the cost of meals, developing menus and other strategic and policy-oriented decisions. The result has been a cooperative venture that even includes incentives for joint investments in cost reduction and quality enhancement programs. In addition, there are schools where the self-operated dining department provides contract food services to other campus units such as the student center. This, too, is a hybrid alternative. The examples described above are intended only to provide an illustration of the variety of choices that are available to an institution. It is important to think creatively about the options available and evaluate each one using the approach described in the guide.

6.1 Conduct Peer Surveys (as needed)

Members of the project team should be assigned the responsibility of surveying the institution's peers to determine how they operate the functional area under consideration and why they chose to do it that way. The peer group selected should include institutions of similar size and mission, institutions with comparable environments and campus cultures and, ideally, institutions which have a reputation for world class operations. In speaking with these institutions, the project team should seek to learn:

- How they operate the functional area (organizational structure, division of responsibility and accountability)

- Why they chose to operate the way they do

- What other ways of operating were considered and why they were rejected

- What they consider to be the greatest strengths and weaknesses of their current approach to operating the functional area.

It should be noted that this activity is not intended to take the place of more detailed site visits and the checking of references that should occur for each proposed vendor or self-operation manager during Phases 8 and 9.

6.2 Consult with Functional Area Professional and Trade Associations

Another source of information that should be drawn upon by the project team is the professional or trade association that represents the functional area being evaluated. These organizations will be especially useful for identifying institutions that have chosen hybrid solutions or that are employing especially creative applications of self-operation. In addition, these associations may assist in identifying the vendors that offer contract services.

6.3 Compile List of Alternatives and Issue a Request for Proposal

The alternatives identified through the peer surveys and professional or trade associations that appear to be reasonable candidates for operating the functional area should be contacted and sent a request for proposal (RFP). The institution need not decide between self-operation or contract management at this time. In fact, it is better if both options are considered simultaneously. The self-operation alternative should be treated like any other vendor and should submit a proposal that outlines its plans for operating the functional area. For institutions that are not currently self-operating, a self-operation spokesperson should be identified from within the institution's business office to prepare an operating proposal. Or, the school should consider hiring an outside consultant to play this role or should seek peer assistance from an equivalent self-operated college. If the institution is interested in pursuing a specific hybrid model, then the RFP should ask both the vendors and the functional manager candidates how they would operate under such an arrangement.

Phase 7 – Review Legal, Ethical, and Community Considerations

Objective: To bring to the decision process an understanding of and a sensitivity to the impact each operating alternative would have on the institution's community (both internal and external) and to understand the levels of liability that each alternative introduces.

An institution cannot effectively choose the best operating model without considering its legal impact as part of the decision process.

This publication provides legal information on many issues which impact the method of operating a campus service. Because this is both a rapidly changing area of the law, and because individual legal jurisdictions are taking different positions on the same or similar issues, it is impossible to definitively address how any specific jurisdiction or branch of government will act. Campuses are urged to use the information provided herein only as a guide. On matters of specific legal interpretation, a campus must gain advice from competent legal counsel and tax consultants.

Institutions face a broad array of legal and ethical issues in the operation of service units that are subject to "privatization." Often, the way in which an institution chooses to operate a functional area determines its legal liability for negligence, defamation, and other tort law. In addition, some operating models can limit the institution's labor law obligations. Similarly, the operational model employed can also impact the institution's tax status and potential for allegations of unfair competition. An institution cannot effectively choose the best operating model for them without considering these legal issues as part of the decision process.

7.1 Determine Impact on Functional Area's Tax Status

Historically, the non-profit status of colleges and universities has exempted their auxiliary services from federal, state, and local income or property taxes. Recently, the tax status of these areas has come under increased scrutiny as governments respond to allegations of unfair competition by small business advocates and seek ways to compensate for revenue shortfalls.

In considering the likely impact of an operating model on the institution's tax status, it is necessary to consider two types of taxes:

- Unrelated Business Income Tax (UBIT)

- Property Tax Exemptions.

In weighing the tax impact of each operating alternative the project team needs to keep in mind that there is nothing wrong with engaging in an activity that is taxable. The project team just needs to consider the likely cost of any change to the institution's tax status brought about by each alternative along with its other benefits and liabilities. It should be noted that throughout this document, discussions of the tax impact of the decision process apply only to U.S. institutions. Currently, Canadian colleges and universities do not face unrelated business income or other tax issues.

Under the concept of unrelated business income tax, income is exempt from taxation if the activity that generates it is substantially related (an activity will be considered substantially related if it contributes in an important way to an organization's exempt purpose) to an organization's exempt purpose or if it meets one of the exceptions or exemptions to UBIT. These exceptions and exemptions include if the function or service 1) is not a trade or business or regularly carried on, 2) essentially all of the labor is voluntary or goods to be sold are donated, 3) has students perform 50% or more of the work as part of an education curriculum, or 4) meets the convenience exemption. The convenience exemption states that income from services or programs that are conducted "for the convenience of students, faculty, and staff is not taxable."

Historically, campuses have made extensive use of the convenience exemption to exempt the income of services and functions like the bookstore or dining services from taxation. The convenience exemption, however, is only applicable to areas that are self-operated. For the purposes of the Internal Revenue Code, once an activity is contracted to another to perform, the issues of substantially related and the convenience exemptions are no longer controlling. Instead, the focus is on the nature of the relationship between the vendor and the institution. If the relationship with the vendor is passive, that is, the institution does not play an active role in the management of the function, then the income will be free of taxation. However, if the institution plays a more active role or is involved in a joint venture with the vendor, then the income is more likely to be seen as taxable by the IRS. Because of this passive/active income dichotomy, the IRS will consider any income received by a campus due to a sharing of profits with the contractor to be unrelated business income. It is the position of the government that if an exempt organization is sharing in net income, it has an interest in the actual management of the service. This interest automatically turns the exempt organization's role into an active one.

As the project team reviews each operating alternative, it must determine what effect each alternative is likely to have on the institution's tax exempt status. Working with an advisor who is familiar with state, federal, and local tax law, the project team needs to determine if alternatives that involve contract management will meet the passive income exemption, or in the case of self-operation, if the functional area will meet the UBIT convenience exemption. Key questions for the project team to consider include:

- Will the institution's financial return for the function be a reimbursement for an identifiable and measurable expense to the campus so as to conform with the passive income exemption?

- Does the institution's desire to maintain a degree of management control over the functional area violate the passive income exemption?

- Will the institution's financial return be paid as a flat dollar amount and/or a percentage of gross income or as a percentage of net income which could be construed as evidence of a joint venture?

- *For self-operation:* Does the operating alternative introduce any services that are not included within the convenience exemption?

It should be noted that if income is found to be unrelated business income under the Internal Revenue Code, the campus may reduce the taxable level of income by the amount of those expenses which are incurred in generating this income. This includes all direct expenses (e.g., labor, cost of goods), as well as an appropriate share of indirect expenses (e.g., insurance, accounting).

A second aspect of the institution's tax exempt status that could be impacted by the contract management/self-operation decision is its exemption from state and local property tax. Increasingly, colleges and universities have seen their property tax exemptions challenged for dual use facilities. These are buildings in which two types of activities occur: those that are clearly educational and those that are considered (at least by local governments) as unrelated to the institution's educational mission. The latter is alleged particularly when the campus uses the space for non-institutional entertainment activities or some other commercial venture. Increasingly, there has been an interest in extending this challenge to include the tax-exempt status of property leased by a campus to a for-profit company to provide services such as the college store or food services. At a minimum, a campus needs to be aware that the use of its facilities by a for-profit corporation (especially high profile national chains) may increase the pressure placed upon the institution to make payments in lieu of taxes.

The Internal Revenue Code specifies that only a limited amount of space in a building funded by exempt bonds may be leased to for-profit organizations. This is one of the areas to be closely examined in the upcoming audits of colleges and universities. Campuses are urged to pay close attention to the outcome of these audits to gain an understanding of how the IRS will interpret this.

7.2 Assess Impact on the Internal and External Community

The self-operation/contract management decision will also have an impact on the local community. This impact carries both a legal and a public relations dimension. The primary legal issue is the impact that any change in operating approach might have on allegations of unfair competition that are aimed at the campus by organizations like the Business Coalition for Fair Competition (BCFC). These organizations seek legislation to regulate all activities in which a non-profit competes with a for-profit. The end goal of these organizations is to have states prohibit non-profits from engaging in any activity that a for-profit is willing to perform. The BCFC clearly states that it sees no difference between a service directly performed by a campus and one that a campus contracts to a for-profit to perform. In considering the pros and cons of choosing an operating model, the institution should keep in mind that contracting for a service will not minimize allegations of unfair competition. In fact, it is possible that contracting for a service will heighten the concerns of the local business community.

The presence of a for-profit corporation may increase the pressure to make payments in lieu of taxes.

In assessing the unfair competition question, the project team should seek advice on the following questions:

- Does your state have an applicable unfair competition/privatization statute? Is such a statute under consideration? Does the State Board of Higher Education and/or the institution's own governing board have an unfair competition policy? Do the policies or the legislation view self-operation any differently than contract management?

- In discussions with the local business community, is there any indication that the service in question may generate unfair competition complaints? Is there a difference in attitude if the service is operated by the institution? by a for-profit organization?

- Is there a way to generate new business for local small businesses by altering how the service is performed without materially altering quality of service, price to the customer, or financial return to the campus?

The concerns of the local business community is just one of the potential impacts on the local community that need to be weighed in choosing an operating method. The project team also needs to consider the institution's historic role in the local community. Institutions in small geographic locales that have historically been a major employer in the community need to anticipate the likely reaction of the community to the introduction of a contract manager. Similarly, urban institutions whose functional areas employ large numbers of minorities must gauge and manage community reaction and perceptions of turning these employees over to a contractor. Even if no employee loses his job or has his compensation reduced, the institution needs to anticipate how the change will be perceived by local government, the press, and community leaders.

The project team also needs to consider the impact that a change in management approach would have on the internal community of students, faculty, and staff. Is one proposed operating model more in keeping with the institution's historic mission and culture than another? What would be a likely impact of introducing a management approach that is counter to the campus culture? Does the institution feel it has an obligation to its employees that would preclude it from entering into a contract management agreement without certain conditions (e.g., full employment, comparable compensation, etc.)?

7.3 Determine Each Alternative's Impact on Legal Liability

The day-to-day operation of a college or university raises a broad range of legal liability issues. These issues are present whether the campus chooses to self-operate a service, contract for its provision, or utilize a combination of the two. Campuses are exposed to negligence claims stemming from on-the-job injuries or on-campus accidents as well as damage suits relating to failure of building or equipment. The key issue that must be weighed in the decision process is how much of the liability that had been the campus's can be transferred to the vendor through contract management or, conversely, what degree of liability that had been the vendor's would have to be assumed by the campus under self-operation. It is important to bear in mind that a campus can never completely transfer its liability for a function or service to a vendor. A portion of the liability will always remain with the institution. In order to manage that liability, the campus needs to diligently monitor the vendor's performance to verify that they are in compliance with all applicable internal and external regulations and guidelines.

The project team needs to consult with the leader of the institution's risk management program during this phase of the decision process. The project team needs to consider how each alternative under consideration would impact the campus's insurance premiums and the likelihood of an increase or decrease in the level of the institution's exposure in the event of a lawsuit. This activity must be performed with an understanding of the operating model developed in Phase 5 of the decision process and the requirements for the degree of institutional control that are described there. The more management control that the campus is seeking in their vision for the functional area's operation, the greater is the campus's potential liability.

A number of tax experts believe that we will see modifications to government policy toward non-profits during the 1990s. Already during this decade the IRS has announced a new standard for reviewing joint ventures, a new standard for corporate sponsorship income, new audit guidelines for exempt hospitals, and the intention to develop new audit guidelines for higher education. Among specific areas that audits of colleges and universities will address are income from contracted services, campus-operated franchises of brand concepts, income from campus-operated services (particularly college stores and food service), and the use of facilities funded by tax-exempt bonds. Campuses are urged to pay close attention to IRS audits of other colleges and universities and to proposed changes in public policy in these areas at all levels of government.

If a campus is going to contract a service, it needs to determine if it can include in the contract the requirement that the vendor bears all federal, state, and local taxes, both those now in existence and those which may be implemented in the future. Also, the institution needs to be aware that if the terms of the contract make the campus a "partner" in the venture, then the courts will look beyond the words of the agreement itself to the actual rights and privileges of the parties.

Phase 8 – Compare and Contrast Proposed Operating Alternatives

Objective: To assess each proposed alternative in terms of the evaluation criteria, to identify the likely trade-offs between each alternative, and to understand the likely impact each alternative would have on the institutional mission and culture, human resources, finances, management control and efficiency, and service quality.

This phase brings together all of the information gathered throughout the decision process to evaluate the alternatives available to the institution for operating the functional area. These alternatives will include self-operation, the proposals from vendors to provide contract management, and, if appropriate, the possibility of providing a hybrid form of operation. The outcome of this phase will be a factual evaluation of the strengths and weaknesses of each alternative and an assessment of the likely impacts on the institution in terms of the decision factors outlined at the beginning of this chapter. Then, by applying the prioritized evaluation criteria adopted in Phase 2 of the process, the optimal solution for the campus will emerge.

8.1 Compare and Contrast Each Alternative to Identify Trade-offs

Each vendor as well as the spokesperson for the self-operation alternative should be asked to submit written documentation and make presentations to the project team that describe how they would operate the functional area. These presentations should address:

- How each party would assist the institution in achieving the vision set forth in the operating model

- What changes each party would make regarding how the function operates to meet customer requirements

- What the human resource policies are of each party, including the utilization of current staff, compensation levels, and staff retention

- How each party would conform with institutional policies and achieve the financial goals and quality standards set by the institution

- What mechanisms would be employed to report their progress, evaluate their performance, and remain accountable to the institution's management.

The ultimate goal of these documents and presentations should be an articulation by the presenters of how the institution would benefit by employing each proposed operating model.

In considering each proposal, the project team should compare and contrast the financial return offered, the level of investment in the infrastructure being proposed, and the impact on the cost of the service to the customer under each proposal. In addition, each proposal needs to be reviewed to determine the level of service quality that will be provided and the range of services that will be offered. It must be consistent with the customer requirements set out in Phase 4. The project team also needs to assess the degree of control that the institution will retain over the functional area. It needs to be sufficient to meet the needs of the institution to control the long-range direction of the functional area's operations. Lastly, the project team should also review the performance and experience of the management teams being proposed in each alternative.

8.2 Identify Legal, Ethical, and Contractual Concerns

Each proposal should be reviewed with the institution's legal staff to determine the impact it will have on the issues of taxation and liability outlined in the previous phase. To the extent possible, the probable impact of each alternative should be quantified. For instance, the change in tax liability or the increase in insurance premiums should be estimated and weighed in any financial comparison of the different alternatives.

The same questions of taxation and legal liability that are asked of potential contract management solutions should also be asked of any proposed self-operation alternatives. For instance, if the institution chooses to self-operate it needs to identify what liability it is taking on and whether it has sufficient insurance. Therefore, the financial impact of any changes necessitated by self-operation to the institution's risk management program should be quantified. Similarly, self-operation alternatives need to be evaluated to determine their impact on the institution's tax status or if they subject the institution to allegations of unfair competition. In short, a proposal to self-operate a function should be evaluated in the same way as a contract management proposal.

From an ethical standpoint each proposal, including self-operation, needs to be evaluated to identify any aspects which are not in keeping with the institution's culture and formal or informal code of business conduct. Areas to focus on as part of this evaluation include human resource policies, the impact on the local business community, and the broader impact each alternative would be likely to have on the campus community.

In the case of contract management, the project team should begin to have preliminary discussions with the vendor to determine the vendor's willingness to agree to contractual provisions that help the institution evaluate the vendor's performance, provides for regular consultations with institution's management and in general supports an open exchange of information that will promote a cooperative partnership with the vendor. Also, the project team should verify that the prospective vendors can meet state and/or institutional standards and requirements regarding vendors.

8.3 Compare and Contrast Intangible Impact of Each Alternative

In addition to the quantitative and qualitative aspect of each alternative, there is a set of intangible costs and benefits that needs to be considered. These intangible issues include:

- Is the proposed operating alternative consistent with the historical mission and culture of the institution?

- What effect will each alternative have on employee morale, both within and outside of the functional area?

- Is the proposed operating alternative likely to increase or decrease the cost or price to the student, faculty, or staff users of the service?

- What will be the effect of each alternative on customer satisfaction?

- Will the operating approach have a positive or negative effect on the institution's relationship with the local business community?

- Will the proposed operating method be sensitive and responsive to the array of students, faculty, and staff that make up the campus community? Will it integrate effectively with the rest of the campus administration?

While these and other issues are not easily quantifiable, they are important to the success of the functional area's operation and need to be considered as part of the decision process. Only the institution knows the history, culture, people, and environment that comprise the campus community and only the institution can determine whether a proposed management approach will function well within it. This is not to say that it would be wrong to choose an operating approach that does not fit perfectly into the campus. Like the other factors in the decision process, these intangible impacts need to be seen as part of the overall analysis of an operating alternative.

8.4 Assess Each Alternative in Terms of the Evaluation Criteria

The final stage of the decision process prior to actually selecting an operating approach is to compare and contrast each alternative using the evaluation criteria developed in Phase 2 as a framework for the comparison. As discussed earlier, the rank-ordered evaluation criteria identify the characteristics and features that are most important to the institution in choosing an operating approach. Each alternative will bring its own unique set of strengths and weaknesses. It is up to the project team to weigh the information that has been gathered about each alternative and to use the evaluation criteria to identify which proposed solution is strongest in the factors that are most important to the institution.

The project team should strive to make the comparative evaluation of each operating alternative as fact-based as possible. To this end, one or two members of the project team should be assigned to each alternative to prepare a summary presentation. For each evaluation criterion, the summary should briefly discuss the proposed solution's likely impact. Each group should present its summary to the project team for consideration and discussion. Based on the information provided in the summaries, the project team should prepare a group summary that ranks each alternative from best to worst for each of the evaluation criteria and should recommend the preferred alternative.

Phase 9 – Select Preferred Alternative

Objective: To select and plan for the implementation of the alternative that best meets the needs of the institution.

At the end of Phase 8, the key decision maker will have a qualitative and quantitative assessment of each alternative, an understanding of the strengths and weaknesses of the current operation, a statement of the mission, long- and short-term goals for the functional area, and the recommendation of the project team of the preferred alternative. Also, the key decision maker will have obtained information as to the potential impact of each alternative on the institution's tax status, liability exposure, and relations with the local community. Lastly, the final piece of information that the decision maker has is a discussion of the intangible impact of each alternative, including its effect on the institution's employees and its sensitivity to and consistency with the campus's historical mission and culture.

While it is not likely that any single element of information will drive the ultimate decision, the cumulative effect should provide the necessary information to select among the alternatives.

9.1 Make Preliminary Selection

Clearly the decision maker is not obligated to choose the alternative that has been recommended by the project team. However, in order to preserve the good will and consensus that has been built by the decision process, the decision maker should be prepared to meet with the project team, present his or her reasons for choosing another alternative, and not finalize the decision until the project team understands and is supportive of the reasoning. Unless this step is taken, the project team members, and by extension the campus community, will no longer have a stake in the selection of the operating alternative and are not likely to be supportive of the decision or of the changes that it is likely to bring about.

9.2 Make Final Arrangements

Prior to formally adopting and announcing a new management approach, there are some final steps that the institution needs to complete. For institutions which have decided to move to or retain contract management, this includes the negotiation of a contract that enumerates the responsibilities of the institution and the vendor in providing the function or service, and puts in place a method for evaluating the vendor's performance. However, the specific elements of contracting for auxiliary services are too numerous and institution-specific to be presented in this guide. While a sample contract has been included as an appendix, we encourage institutions only to use this as a starting point in their negotiations and to seek the advice and input of legal counsel in the negotiation of the actual contract.

For institutions that have chosen to move to or retain self-operation, this activity includes the hiring and negotiation of contracts with the individuals that will make up the functional area's management team. Similar to the negotiations with a vendor, the agreements reached with individual managers should include the institution's expectations for performance as well as incentives for reaching and exceeding the institution's goals and objectives for the functional area.

Institutions that are seeking to put a hybrid (self-operation and contract management) operating model in place will need to perform both of the steps outlined above. In this case, careful attention needs to be paid to the division of responsibilities and authority between the vendor and the institutional personnel.

9.3 Transition to a New Operating Approach

For institutions that have selected a new operating approach, a transition plan needs to be developed that establishes the schedule for moving from current management to the new operation. Elements of a transition plan often include the verification of inventories, preliminary employee training, and the announcement to and education of the institutional community about the change. The transition period should also be utilized to address the concerns and questions of the functional area's current staff. New management should meet individually and collectively with each staff member to discuss changes in job responsibility, performance expectations, professional development opportunities, and other issues surrounding employee compensation and benefits.

Institutions that have chosen to retain their current operating approach should see this time as an opportunity for a fresh start for the functional area. This opportunity should be used by the functional area to redefine to its customers its role and responsibilities, to introduce new services or initiatives to improve quality and contain costs, and to demonstrate a willingness and a plan to address any previous shortcomings. The institution should inform the campus community that the current management team was the winner in a competitive process to choose the best operating approach for the institution. These steps will stem criticism that the current management is a monopoly that is taking advantage of the campus community and will demonstrate management's commitment to improving the service that the functional area provides.

Phase 10 – Establish Continuous Improvement and Assessment Process

Objective: To put in place an ongoing process to assess the functional area's performance, to promote accountability, and to identify opportunities to continuously improve the functional area.

The campus community and administration need to continue to play an active role in assessing the functional area's performance.

Whether the institution chooses self-operation, contract management, or some combination, the process does not end with the transition to the new management. The campus community and the institution's administration need to continue to play an active role in assessing the functional area's performance (especially its progress toward the goals and objectives established during the decision process) in monitoring its financial performance, in measuring customer satisfaction, and in identifying opportunities for improving the functional area's operation.

The institution may want to consider charging the project team with the responsibility for managing the continuous improvement process. The project team would be well suited for this role because of its broad representation from the campus community and the knowledge of the functional area that it gained during the decision process. This group could work with the functional area manager to periodically administer customer satisfaction surveys, to monitor the functional area's progress toward achieving the operating model developed during the decision process, and to identify new initiatives to improve efficiency and quality. In cases of contract management, this group could also be given responsibility for monitoring the terms of the agreement with the vendor. Finally, for both contract management and self-operation, the group could perform an annual formal evaluation of the functional area's performance in terms of the evaluation criteria used in the selection process. The team could then issue a report to the functional area manager and the campus administration that identifies where the function is performing well and where it is falling below the institution's expectations. Specific recommendations could then be prepared in conjunction with the functional area manager to improve performance in areas of weakness.

To facilitate the day-to-day interactions between a vendor and the institution, a single member of the institution's staff should be designated to serve as a contract administrator/vendor liaison. It would be this person's responsibility to monitor the vendor's performance and adherence to the guidelines, requirements, and performance measures agreed to in the contract. While this individual needs to have some understanding of the functional areas of operation, it is not necessary, nor would it be cost effective, to replicate the skill set of the functional area manager. Finally, the level of effort required to perform such a job would not require a full-time commitment.

Chapter III.

Functional Decision Process

While the approach presented in Chapter II provides a framework for the self-operation/ contract management decision that can be used for any function, there are unique considerations and emphases that are introduced when the decision process is applied to a particular functional area. For each of the functions and services that this study focused on, we found that although the decision factors remain the same, their relative importance and complexity vary. For instance, issues of taxation are of great importance in deciding how to operate a campus bookstore or dining service, but are of relatively little importance in determining how to operate the campus security. Likewise, the potential for liability is often a driving force in child care decisions, but plays a minor role in administrative computing.

Chapter III will review each of the six functional areas in terms of the decision factors (financial, human resources, mission and culture, management control and efficiency, service quality, and legal and ethical considerations) to highlight the unique aspects of each function that are most important in making the self-operation/contract management decision. Wherever possible, the decision-making framework will be tailored to assist in assessing each functional area. For each functional area, a decision matrix has been provided that presents on a single page the phases of the decision process, the decision factors, and the unique issues and consideration that characterize the decision process for the functional area under consideration. The matrix links the data collection phases of the decision process to the decision factors by pointing out the unique aspects of each functional area.

Facilities

The operation of a facilities department involves a series of contract management/self-operation decisions that are made on an almost daily basis. For each new construction, renovation, or maintenance project, the facilities manager must determine if his staff has the skills and available time to perform the project or whether he needs to hire a contractor to complete the work. Also, he must determine which alternative offers the optimum balance between quality and cost. These same factors are important in considering whether to utilize contract management to operate all or part of a facilities department.

Decision Matrix

Functional Area: Facilities

Decision Factor \ Decision Process	Identify Key Participants	Develop Analytical Framework	Assess the Current Environment	Identify Customer Requirements	Develop Solution Design	Identify Solution Alternatives	Review Legal, Ethical, and Community Considerations
Financial	• Facilities Audit Specialist		• Energy Cost • HVAC, Electrical & Plumbing				
Human Resources	• Labor Relations • Union Representative		• Employee Skill Sets	• Employee Training Programs • Planned Expansion of Plant			• Number of minority and/or employees from local community
Mission & Culture				• Balance between quality and cost			
Management Control & Efficiency			• Skill of Current Director		• Preventive Maintenance Programs • Performance Measures	• Hybrid-Contract for Director only or just one aspect of operation, e.g., custodial	
Service Quality		• Work Order Turnaround Time • Frequency of Repeated Repairs	• Current Relationship of Department to Campus				
Legal & Ethical Considerations			• Do current contractual obligations preclude the use of a vendor?				• Who will be financially liable for injuries or property damage

Financial

In assessing the financial aspects of the decision, it is important to look beyond the day-to-day operational costs of the department and to include such financial considerations as:

- Required investment necessary to complete any deferred maintenance

- Level of investment required to replace or upgrade HVAC, electrical, plumbing, and other building systems

- Energy costs

- Growth in employee compensation packages.

As part of the assessment of current operations, it can be very beneficial to perform a facilities audit of the campus to determine the existing level of deferred maintenance. Also, discussions with vendors should include the possibility of a shared investment to upgrade or replace the department's equipment. These steps will enable the institution to have a more complete picture of the financial aspects of each operating alternative.

Human Resources

The impact on human resources is a major consideration in making the contract management/self-operation decision. Considerations in this area should include:

- Is the department unionized? Does the current contract allow the school to introduce contract management? What would be the likely impact of contract management on other unionized areas of the campus?

- How adequate is the current level of employee training? Does the vendor offer training programs that the school can not? How valuable to the department's operations would this training be?

- Does the department employ a large number of minority employees? In light of this, would contract management expose the university to an unacceptable level of adverse publicity?

In cases where unions are involved, it is important to include the institution's labor negotiators as members of the decision-making team. Also, union leadership from the facilities area and other functional areas will have to be brought into the process if the institution is considering a contract management arrangement. This will help to minimize any fear or distrust that may be brought about by the consideration of contract management (staff reductions, pay cuts, new boss, etc.) and help to prevent any labor interruptions.

Mission and Culture

In order to choose the right operating model for a facilities department, it is necessary to first adopt a clear set of goals and expectations for the department. These goals and expectations will help the facilities department to determine the set of services that it needs to offer to the community and will help in striking a balance between the need to perform high-quality work and the need to control costs.

Management Control & Efficiency

The capabilities of the current management team are central to the self-operation/contract management decision for facilities. The complexity of facilities operations requires a director who is strong technically as well as being a financial and human resource manager. The school must realistically evaluate its ability to recruit and retain quality managers for the department. As part of this evaluation, the school should undertake a review of the compensation packages being offered to facilities managers both within and outside of the higher education industry in their area.

In considering the possibility of contract management, the institution needs to carefully evaluate the implication of giving a degree of control over the function to the vendor.

For example:

■ Will the priorities of the vendor and the institution coincide or is the vendor more likely to place a greater emphasis on short-term objectives at the expense of long-term goals? What implications does this have for the school's ability to maintain and enhance the condition of the physical plant?

■ What performance measures can be built into the contract to hold vendors accountable for the quality of the work they perform without robbing them of their management flexibility?

Service Quality

In addition, in choosing an operating model for the facilities area, consideration needs to be given to the relationship between the department and the school community. In cases where there has been a strong collaborative relationship, the institution needs to decide whether the presence of an outside vendor would harm or enhance this relationship. Conversely, in cases where the department is perceived as being unresponsive or too costly, the institution needs to decide if a self-operated department can be successful.

Specific things to look at when judging the service quality of a facilities department include:

■ Turnaround time for work orders

■ Frequency of cost or schedule overruns on maintenance and construction projects

■ Instances of repeated requests for the same repair.

Legal & Ethical

The legal and liability issues that need to be considered in the contract management/ self-operation decision for the facilities function focus on the trade-off of accountability between the institution and the vendor. Specific legal and ethical concerns introduced in the facilities area include:

■ Who will be responsible for employee injuries? Who will provide training on the use of hazardous machinery or chemicals?

■ Who will be financially responsible for income lost in the dining rooms or bookstore or for damage to research projects due to equipment failure or an error by a facilities staff member?

- Who will be liable for injury to individuals from a slip and fall on an uncleared path, shelving not appropriately constructed, a disease transmitted due to improper treatment of drinking water, or other injuries that occur due to employee negligence or equipment malfunction?

- Who is responsible for compliance with facilities related local, state, and federal regulations?

Bookstore

The bookstore represents a functional area where the potential for financial return is quite high if the store is well run. At the same time, the bookstore is closely identified with the institution's academic mission and institutional image. The challenge facing administrators is to choose an operating approach that will enable the institution to realize the store's revenue potential and remain sensitive both to students' concerns over the price of course supplies and to faculty who often view the bookstore as an extension of the library and an integral part of the school's academic programs.

Financial

In considering the financial aspects of the self-operation/contract management decision for a bookstore, it is important to include:

For self-operation

- The opportunity cost of maintaining an inventory

- The potential income lost due to store's provision of free or subsidized services, and discounted or "at cost" sales in support of the institution and its objectives

- Contributions to the institution in excess of normal business expenses (e.g., scholarship fund, student government association, etc.) which are recorded as fund transfers rather than as a distribution of profits

- The potential for, and loss experience, for inventory that is no longer salable (out of publication, no longer in use on campus)

- The personnel cost to recruit and retain a high-quality store manager and staff

- The cost of providing support services to the bookstore (e.g., accounting services, purchasing, accounts payable, receiving) vs. the administrative or other charges paid for these services

- The potential investment required to periodically renovate and modernize the store to maintain it as a positive advertisement for the institution.

For contract management

- The potential to free cash by selling the store inventory vs. the write-off of value not recovered

- The revenue stream being offered by the vendor vs. the potential revenue being foregone should the store's performance exceed expectations, or if significant sales are excluded from institutional participation by the agreement, or if the contract fails to keep pace with inflation.

Decision Matrix

Functional Area: Bookstore

Decision Process \ Decision Factor	Identify Key Participants	Develop Analytical Framework	Assess the Current Environment	Identify Customer Requirements	Develop Solution Design	Identify Solution Alternatives	Review Legal, Ethical, and Community Considerations
Financial	▪ Individual familiar with retail operation and accounting	▪ Financial goals: revenue vs. price	▪ Cost vs. recoverable value of existing inventory	▪ Cost of Required improvements to store to enhance services	▪ Cost to recruit or retain quality store manager		
Human Resources			▪ Ability to provide incentives/career path to store manager			▪ Need for management continuity	
Mission & Culture		▪ Projects appropriate image		▪ Provide maximum value at reasonable cost	▪ Multi-purpose store or extension of library	▪ Operating model consistent with culture of campus	
Management Control & Efficiency		▪ Accomplishes current mission, goals, and institutional expectations	▪ Adequacy of Retail Systems ▪ Condition of Current Store Facilities	▪ Need for faculty, student and staff input into operation decisions			
Service Quality		▪ Learning materials available when needed		▪ Range of services			▪ Proximity of local stores
Legal & Ethical Considerations				▪ Need to require or exclude sale of certain merchandise			▪ UBIT, Property Tax, Unfair competition

- The cash outlay savings to the institution of an investment made or shared by the vendor to improve the store facilities vs. the reduction in annual income and contract length as the contractor recoups his investment

- The investment and cash outlay required by the institution to go back to self-operation (repurchase inventory, hire staff, etc.).

Human Resources

The human resource issues that are especially important when choosing an operating model for a bookstore focus primarily on the store manager. Most of the individuals we contacted cited the capabilities of the store manager as the most critical factor in the ultimate success or failure of the store. Therefore, in the decision process the institution must carefully consider the quality of the manager that the institution has or can hire vs. the quality of the manager that the vendor will provide. Key questions to consider include:

- Will the vendor provide a single store manager or will they rotate managers during the life of the contract?

- Would having several managers be detrimental to employee morale and performance, and would it make the store any less responsive to the campus community? What have other schools' experiences been with the vendor under consideration in regard to the quality and consistency of store management?

- What is the likelihood that the school could retain a single store manager throughout the same time frame if it self-operated? Would there be a benefit to having more than one manager? Would the cost of retaining a single manager outweigh the benefits?

- What incentives (e.g., career path, financial rewards, etc.) can the institution provide to the manager of a self-operated store to improve the store's performance and to meet and exceed the institution's goals and expectations for the store?

- Does the contract company's method of performance evaluation for management and staff fit the philosophy of the institution and its goals and expectations for the store? Will the institution have input into the manager's performance evaluation?

Another major issue involves staff training and development to effectively understand and operate a retail operation. For both self-operated and contracted stores, effectiveness indicators include the availability of needed merchandise, level of service, employee responsiveness, product merchandising, and the overall attractiveness of the store as a place to shop.

Mission & Culture

A central issue regarding mission and culture for a bookstore is profit. Does the institution see the store's primary objective as income contribution, or is the primary mission to provide learning materials to students at the lowest reasonable cost, earning little profit (with occasional losses a possibility)? Regardless of whether the store is self-operated or managed by a contractor, the institution needs to consistently define where on the revenue vs. lower price trade-off it expects the store to operate.

The need to choose an operating approach that projects an image that is consistent with the institution's culture is especially important for bookstores because of their high visibility. Every student and faculty member makes repeated contact with the bookstore and is more aware of how it is operated than most other functional areas. In addition, the bookstore is often a link for the institution to both alumni and prospective students who shop there during campus visits. Therefore, choosing an operating approach which presents an image that is inconsistent with the school's mission and culture will be very evident to the majority of these groups, and is likely to elicit a more vocal response than in other functional areas.

Because many initial contracts include a refurbishing of the store, one test of how well contracting maintains an image reflecting the mission and culture of the institution is to visit and evaluate bookstores that have been contracted for five, eight, ten, or more years. Does the image projected by these stores reflect the current mission and culture of the institutions they serve?

Finally, the mission and culture of the bookstore is changing as the role of technology has grown on campus. Many campuses have already seen a number of changes brought about by technology, including:

■ Faculty turning to custom publishing because textbooks cannot keep up with the information explosion in economics, politics, and science

■ Evolution of a new publishing model, taking the printing process closer to the customer through digital reproduction

■ A revolution in the way that text and other media are created, stored, and delivered and the growth of multimedia through the use of computers

■ Powerful computer-based networks, such as Internet, becoming standard communication channels.

These developments will affect the relationship between stores and their customers and are broadening the college store's role on campus. In developing the mission for its campus bookstore, an institution needs to consider the growing partnership being fostered by technology between the bookstore and faculty, campus print shops, and the campus computing center. For instance, partnerships between stores and campus print shops are evolving to facilitate the purchase of and optimize the use of expensive production equipment. Therefore, in choosing an operating model for the bookstore, an institution needs to evaluate:

■ Whether an operating alternative has demonstrated success in bringing technology to the campus through the bookstore

■ Whether potential technology partners, such as computer hardware companies, established relationships with a contract management or self-operation leader that would benefit the institution

■ Whether each operating alternative adequately supports the development and distribution of courseware by faculty and the use of electronic networks such as Internet to communicate and consult with faculty and students.

Management Control & Efficiency

The operation of a bookstore is quite unlike any of the other functions that most institutions have historically dealt with. As a retail operation, the bookstore requires information systems for effective inventory control, policies and procedures to control inventory and protect the institution from fraud and theft, and management skills in marketing and customer service. The school must candidly assess its ability to provide these tools and techniques for the bookstore as well as the cost of providing them.

While the school should assess a vendor's ability to provide these tools and techniques as well, it is equally important to assess the vendor's performance at other institutions. Are modern, state-of-the-art information systems in use? If not, why? Are the students, faculty, and staff satisfied with the merchandising and service that these systems facilitate?

Service Quality

As mentioned earlier, the high visibility of the campus bookstore subjects its operations to very close scrutiny. The store's responsiveness to the campus community is of tantamount importance to its success. In specifying its expectations for the store's performance from either a vendor or an in-house manager, the institution should address considerations such as: the store schedule of operating hours, how the peak sales periods at term openings should be handled (increased hours and staff, maximum wait at checkout, etc.), and the range of services to be provided by the store.

The bookstore is looked upon to provide a wide range of services to the campus that go beyond selling books and school supplies. Often, the campus also requires the bookstore to be a grocery store, drug store, or even a small department store. The institution must work with the store's customers to define the range of services that they require from the bookstore and to determine the quality of those services. This is especially true of rural campuses where off-campus shopping alternatives are geographically remote.

Finally, the institution needs to evaluate the alternatives in terms of the initiatives that are being proposed to control the cost of course materials to students. Will they work with faculty to develop course packs (locally produced anthologies or other tailored packages of information from a variety of sources)? Do they have an effective used-book program (use multiple suppliers as well as repurchase from students)? Can they provide specialized course supplies (laboratory, art, drafting, cooking) at competitive prices?

Legal & Ethical

Issues of taxation are the primary legal concern that impacts the decision process for bookstores. The institution needs to consider that if it decides to self-operate then it must comply with the IRS guidelines for unrelated business income tax: "The IRS has recently found that the sale of required classroom materials; trade books; items with campus logos, marks, or name on them; school supplies; low-cost novelty items; high-demand convenience items; records; tapes; and the like are exempt from taxation. As items take on a useful life of more than one year and seem to have no relation to higher education per se, the advice is that they will be taxable. In this group, one finds watches, higher priced gift items and apparel, appliances, plants, and similar tangible goods" (Bookman, M. *Protecting Your Organization's Tax Exempt Status: A Guide For Non-Profit Managers*, San Francisco, Jossey-Bass Publishers, Inc., 1992).

If a campus decides to contract its college store, the income tax issue totally changes. The focal question becomes how the payment to the campus is calculated. If the payment meets the passive income requirements, there will be no tax consequences. That is, the institution must play a passive role in the management of the operation and cannot participate in any joint ventures with the vendor. If income is found to be taxable, the campus will pay a tax based upon the total amount of unrelated business income minus all allowable expenses. All expenses directly associated with generating this income are clearly deductible. It is with indirect expenses that campuses may face a difficulty. The IRS requires the campus to show that it has a reasonable accounting process for dividing these indirect expenses between taxable and nontaxable activities. A university was challenged in a recent audit on how it divided these indirect expenses. It attempted to include a percentage of the cost for managing the entire academic program. The IRS said that it could only include those administrative costs which are needed for the specific activity which generates the unrelated business income.

Other legal issues to consider include, whether to require or exclude the sale of certain merchandise by contract managed stores and what types of merchandise that a vendor has the exclusive right to sell. The scope of the vendor's exclusive sales right impacts sales by student organizations, other campus support organizations, other campus departments, and contractors (e.g., alumni associations, athletic concessions, food service), licensing agreements, and potential new ventures in the future. There is also the question as to whether the vendor will be required to provide certain services (e.g., computer sales and support services, check cashing, postal supplies) which are typically not profitable. Conversely, some schools do not want certain goods sold on campus (e.g., tobacco products, pornographic materials). If the campus wants the option to exclude product lines, it must so specify in its contract with the vendor.

Finally, unfair competition questions for either self-operated or contracted stores must be examined based on the local political climate and state laws. A number of campuses have found unanticipated opposition from local vendors to a privatized campus store. These vendors fear that the new operator will have a more aggressive marketing approach, will expand product lines, and may be able to underprice them. Campuses need to closely gauge their local community on this issue. Institutionally operated stores have also been confronted by unfair competition claims. The most prevalent form of these claims has been with computer sales, particularly where the campus does not restrict sales to academically related needs.

Dining Services

Like the campus bookstore, dining services are a highly visible campus function whose operations draw a great degree of scrutiny. Dining services have perhaps the largest diversity of customers, ranging from a freshman student to a foreign graduate student to the president of the institution. Each of these customers has different needs and expectations for the dining service program, making it especially challenging to select an operating approach that meets all the needs. Further challenging the manager is the fact that on some campuses, dining services must compete with private restaurants and fast food chains in the local community.

Financial

In assessing the costs of self-operation/contract management for food services, it is necessary to paint as complete a picture of the total costs as possible. For institutions that are currently self-operating, it is important to include the support costs for the functional area such as accounting and purchasing. Also, the institution should take into account any money it already spends for contracted food services, such as catering, that would be provided by a vendor under contract management. Finally, it is necessary to consider if student meal plan fees are being used to subsidize the operating costs of any other campus functions.

For contract management, it is important to look beyond the revenue that they derive from the contract to also take into account the money they save from not having to pay employee wages and benefits. Also, the costs associated with bidding, negotiating, and administering the contract on an ongoing basis need to be considered. It is also important to take into account any investments that have been made in the infrastructure of dining services, including any interest-free loans to the institution. These investments must be weighed against any reduction in annual income and contract length that occurs as the vendor recoups his investment. Finally, the institution needs to consider the investment and cash outlay required by the institution to move back to self-operation (repurchase inventory, hire staff, etc.).

Human Resources

The major human resource related issue to consider is the institution's ability to offer compensation packages to dining service managers and staff that are competitive with those being offered in the local private sector market place. To facilitate this analysis, the school should contact national food service agencies both within the higher education industry

(National Association of College & University Food Services [NACUFS]) as well as in other industries which are active in the area. In this way they will be able to gain some sense of the investment required to retain a manager with the qualifications they seek.

The presence of labor unions on the campus adds another dimension to the human resource aspect of the contract management decision. A campus with a unionized dining service staff that self-operates needs to carefully consider what effect introducing contract management would have on their labor relations. As part of the decision process, these campuses need to meet with the union leadership and explain how contract management would affect staffing levels, compensation packages, and the present union agreements before selecting an operating approach. Failure to do this raises the likelihood that the campus will experience a work stoppage by its campus labor unions. Related to this issue, the institution needs to consult with its legal advisors to determine if anything in its present union contracts precludes it from utilizing contract management in dining services.

The campus also needs to weigh the impact that a change in operating might have on student employees in dining services. The institution needs to consider whether its students would be any more or less willing to work for a self-operated food service as opposed to one that is contracted. Would the vendor be willing to subsidize the student's wages? What might be the net effect in the levels of student employment on the campus?

Mission & Culture

Having a clear sense of the dining services mission as well as its role in achieving and supporting the goals and objectives of the institution will help balance the trade-off between quality and cost. Quality is an elusive characteristic to define for food. The variety of individuals that are served by campus food services all come with their own cultural and regional food experiences and their own individual opinions about what is "good" food. Whether the campus chooses self-operation, contract management, or a hybrid approach, it needs to establish the standard for food quality that must be met. In order to select the right level of quality, the institution needs to weigh such factors as the rate of return it requires for its food service investment, the importance of food services in student satisfaction and retention, and the number and type of campus events that are catered by the food services department. For instance, institutions in the midst of capital campaigns that require a higher level of catered campus functions will likely seek different types of menu items than an institution that only has a few catered events per year. For the former, the added cost incurred is seen as an investment in the institution's development activities.

Similarly, it is also important for the institution to define the financial mission of its dining service operation. Specifically, the institution must determine whether the primary objective of dining services is income contribution or providing quality food services to students at the lowest reasonable cost. Without a clear articulation of expectations for the financial performance of its dining services, the institution will be at a disadvantage in selecting between contract management and self-operation.

Many institutions consider the mission of the institution to include purchasing products from small businesses and/or women- or minority-owned businesses. In this case, the institution needs to determine if a vendor will abide by this policy or if self-operation presents a better opportunity for purchasing from these businesses. Finally, the institution should consider visiting campuses that have employed contract management for a significant period of time (5 to 10 years) to evaluate how well these operations have been tailored to reflect the mission and culture of the schools they serve. A similar evaluation could also be performed of self-operated dining services.

Decision Matrix

Functional Area: Dining Services

Decision Process / Decision Factor	Identify Key Participants	Develop Analytical Framework	Assess the Current Environment	Identify Customer Requirements	Develop Solution Design	Identify Solution Alternatives	Review Legal, Ethical, and Community Considerations
Financial			• Cost of Central Administration Support Services or Contract Administration			• Which alternative would be able to purchase supplies for less	
Human Resources			• Ability to hire and retain manager				• Current obligations to work force under union contracts
Mission & Culture			• Number of mission critical initiatives supported by Food Services	• Level of food quality balanced against cost			
Management Control & Efficiency		• Cost per meal served • Participation Rate				• Hybrid Alternatives	
Service Quality	• Identify all of Dining Service Customers	• Customer Satisfaction Surveys		• Quality and variety of menu choices			• Competition from local community
Legal & Ethical Considerations			• Exclusive Right clauses in agreements with current food service vendors		• Potential change in tax status	• Potential Transfer of liability to vendor	• Adherence to alcoholic beverage control regulations

Management Control & Efficiency

An important aspect of operational efficiency to assess for dining services is whether a vendor offers the campus purchasing efficiencies that self-operation would not. For instance, can a vendor purchase food for a lower cost than a self-operated dining service could because of the volume discounts it enjoys? Will those savings be passed along to the institution? Does the institution currently receive discounts on purchase from local suppliers because of its non-profit status that might not be extended to a corporate food service operator? What impact would this have on total operating costs? Finally, can a vendor purchase a wider range of products because of a nationwide purchasing operation? Would any savings be offset by higher shipping and/or storage costs? Are there regional buying groups that your campus could participate in to achieve the same advantages?

To answer these questions, some campuses have sought bids from area suppliers and calculated the cost of purchasing supplies for their food services based on their current usage levels. They then asked vendors to provide as part of their proposals an estimate of the cost for the same sample of goods if the institution contracted with the vendor. In addition, one institution we spoke with played a leadership role in establishing a regional buying group of the self-operated dining services in their geographic locale.

Other measures of efficiency that can be utilized in assessing the performance of a food service operation include:

- Sales per labor hour/cost
- Cost per meal served
- Participation rate — percentage of students eligible for a meal that are actually served
- General student satisfaction as measured through periodically administered surveys.

In weighing the potential impact of contract management on management control, it is important to ascertain if the investment priorities of the vendor can be made to coincide with the institutions. For instance, is the vendor more likely to place greater emphasis on short-term objectives at the expense of long-term goals? What implications might this have for the school's ability to maintain and enhance the condition of equipment, maintenance, and facilities?

Service Quality

In addressing the issue of service quality, it is important to define all of the customers of food services on your campus. It is important to include such users as the president's office and conference center, which rely on food services to cater high profile events that produce revenue for the institution or promote the institution's image. For some campuses, the ability of an operating alternative to meet the quality needs of this group is as important as meeting the needs of the larger student population (see Mission & Culture discussion above). Also, it is important to keep in mind that the definition of quality requirements includes not just the menu, but also the ambience within which the meal is served.

Through the process of defining quality expectations, the institution should also identify any specialized menu needs that a customer group may have. For instance, if the campus has a large number of vegetarians, foreign students, or commuter students, it may require menu selections that are different from the standard campus menu. The ability of a vendor or self-operation to meet these needs and the resulting impact on the cost of providing food services is an important factor in the decision process.

In defining the scope and quality of the services that they require from either self-operation or a vendor, the institution must also take into account a number of operational issues. The hours and days of operation required of dining services will have a significant impact on operating costs and need to be defined explicitly in the operating model constructed in Phase 5 of the decision process. In addition, the campus needs to enumerate the type and variety of services it requires to support campus activities, including catering, delivery, concessions, fast food, fine dining, hotels, and conference centers. The ability of each solution alternative to provide the mix of services required by your campus can then be evaluated in detail during Phase 8 of the decision process.

Finally, the institution must determine a set of standards for public health and sanitation to which a vendor or self-operation manager will be held. Further, the institution should specify how it will monitor dining services' performance against these standards. In the case of contract management, it should be made clear that the vendor is responsible for adhering to all state, local, and institutional guidelines.

Legal & Ethical

The legal aspect of the decision process for dining services focuses on the transfer of liability between a vendor and the institution for such instances as food poisoning or incidents stemming from the consumption of alcoholic beverages. Other issues include the impact of introducing a contractor on campus on the presence of other current or future vendors who provide catering, sales at athletic events, or outlets of national food service franchises. Will the presence of one vendor preclude the institution from using another vendor or self-operation for another aspect of their food services?

Some of the liability issues associated with dining services can be transferred to the vendor if the school chooses contract management. Similarly, if an institution moves from contract management to self-operation it will have to reassume those liabilities and need to assess the added cost it would incur for risk management. In either scenario, the institution needs to be aware that in case of an incident, the public looks to the campus as the responsible party irrespective of operating mode. As mentioned earlier in the guide, a residual liability will always remain with the institution. In order to manage this liability, the institution needs to proactively monitor the vendor's adherence to all applicable regulations and guidelines.

A particular risk management issue for food services is alcoholic beverages. The campus needs to be certain that all risk associated with this service can be transferred to the vendor should it choose to contract. The campus may also want to ascertain if the vendor follows appropriate alcohol beverage control regulations for its jurisdiction.

Food services departments face tax and unfair competition concerns very similar to college stores. As long as the convenience exemption is in place, it is very important that the campuses which self-operate separate sales to students, faculty, and staff from all other sales. If this does not occur, the IRS can take the position that none of the sales falls within this exception. (Note: In many jurisdictions, the campus needs this detail for sales tax purposes.) Sales to other classes of persons may not be taxable if the sale is substantially related to the organization's exempt purpose. A second UBIT issue deals with food sales off campus. The IRS looks at all such sales as suspect. This is particularly true if the clientele are not regular members of the campus community.

The potential levy of a property tax bill should a campus contract for its food service must be recognized. This is true whether the campus only contracts with a specified brand concept or for one or more components of its food services program. Campuses are advised to protect themselves by having the vendor agree to assume the cost of taxes which might be imposed during the term of the contract.

Administrative Computing

For purposes of this illustration, we have chosen to discuss the decision process only as it applies to administrative computing. However, administrative computing is only a subset of a much broader functional area: information technology. Information technology includes academic and administrative computing, telecommunications, networking, and graphic and media services. Recently, colleges and universities have been focusing on this broader set of functional areas in evaluating contract management or self-operation alternatives. Further, the IT area lends itself to a number of hybrid alternatives including:

- The operation of a functional subset of IT (e.g., administrative computing, telecommunications, etc.)

- A specific administrative computing system (e.g., admissions, development, etc.)

- Conversion of one hardware and/or operating system software environment to another

- Hardware and/or software maintenance services.

Finance

Because of the fast pace at which technology changes and must be replaced to stay current, required short- and long-term investment is an important aspect of the financial assessment of any operating alternative. The institution must identify the likely investment needed for both hardware and software if it self-operates and compare that to the cost of upgrading the technology over the same period under each vendor proposal. Another cost associated with the fast pace of technology changes is training. Many schools look at contracting as a short-term opportunity to acquire training for its employees that it couldn't otherwise afford.

In assessing its ongoing operating costs for computing, the school needs to include the money it is currently paying to vendors and consultants to maintain its hardware and software and identify which of those costs could be covered by a vendor under contract management and which costs would still be borne by the school. Finally, if the need to implement new systems is in part driving the self-operation/contract management decision, then the school should also assess the costs of acquiring and implementing new systems if they continue to self-operate.

Human Resources

The institution needs to objectively assess the capabilities of its in-house staff to determine if they have the skills in place to maintain the types of technology that the school foresees utilizing in the current decade. If the necessary skills are not present, then the institution needs to determine the cost of acquiring those skills through hiring of new staff or through contracting with a vendor to provide those missing skills. In the case of contract management, the institution needs to determine how it would manage the transfer of operations back to the institution from the vendor. The mission critical nature of administrative computing makes it imperative that a contingency plan be in place for staffing and operating the administrative computing center in the event that the contract with a vendor is terminated.

Decision Matrix

Functional Area: Administrative Computing

Decision Factor \ Decision Process	Identify Key Participants	Develop Analytical Framework	Assess the Current Environment	Identify Customer Requirements	Develop Solution Design	Identify Solution Alternatives	Review Legal, Ethical, and Community Considerations
Financial			• Include current payments to maintain hardware	• Cost and benefit of updating technology & software	• Cost of training staff to support new technology		
Human Resources			• How up-to-date are the skills of current staff			• What will happen to employees without the skills to support a vendor's products	
Mission & Culture				• Can a vendor's employee support the needs of campus users	• Is solution consistent with long-term technology strategy		
Management Control & Efficiency			• Do current staff have skill and time to implement new systems			• Does vendor offer proven methodology to limit campus risk	
Service Quality			• How is academic computing supported?	• Do vendor's products meet user's needs	• Who will provide PC Training & Support		
Legal & Ethical Considerations				• What levels of security are required	• Who has responsibility for data integrity		• Copyrights/responsibility for upgrading software

46

Mission & Culture

It is critical that the institution selects an operating approach that is consistent with its strategic technology plan. It would not benefit the institution if it selected an operating approach that introduced technologies that were not consistent with the direction the institution is headed in. Likewise, the institution would not want to employ an operating approach that would not cost-effectively support the types of initiatives and products that make up the campus administrative computing strategy. Finally, the campus decision makers must determine which operating alternative provides the fastest, most cost-effective, and least risky way of achieving their strategic technology objectives.

The nature of today's integrated information systems requires that the individuals who support those systems come in contact with a broad base of users from around the campus. These users often include all of the major administrative functions on campus as well as academic departments and student support services. The campus must determine if introducing a vendor would be disruptive to these relationships. Or, does self-operation provide a cost-effective way to provide the diverse set of services required by the broad user groups?

Management Control & Efficiency

The information contained on the campus computer system is as much an asset of the institution as the building that it is contained in. As such, the institution has a financial stake in maintaining and safeguarding that asset. Therefore, as in the facilities area, the campus must select an operating model that enables it to maintain enough control over the management and priority-setting of the department to ensure the maintenance of those assets. Questions that the project team should be asking throughout the decision process include:

- Can a vendor operate the department more efficiently through its methodologies and training programs?

- Does the institution have on its staff an individual with sufficient time and expertise to monitor a vendor contract? Can such a person be hired? At what cost?

- What will happen to employees who do not have the skills to support new products that are introduced by the vendor — retraining, outplacement?

- If the current systems need to be replaced, does the current administrative computing staff have the skills and the available time to select and implement the new systems or would the institution need to hire a contractor anyway?

- Is the vendor offering to replace the current hardware and software with new products? Do those products meet the campus's functional and technical needs?

Service Quality

An important point regarding consideration of contract management or self-operation for administrative computing is that administrative computing is no longer a function that can operate relatively independently, in isolation from the rest of the campus community. The most successful administrative computing organizations function in partnership with their users, understanding not just the technical aspects of their jobs but also the overall mission, goals, and objectives of the institution.

Therefore, it is important to understand the types of services the entire campus needs from the administrative computing function. Important questions to ask include:

■ How sophisticated are the users? Do they require extensive training? Have they successfully integrated technology into the way they do business?

■ Do administrative departments require PC training and support? Who will provide it under the proposed operating alternative?

■ Who supports academic computing needs on your campus? Are there any efficiencies that can be gained by combining parts of it with administrative computing under the new operating model? Does this introduce new requirements? Which operating model is best equipped to meet them?

In addition to deciding whether or not to contract for the operation of its administrative computing function, the institution needs to determine if the hardware and software products offered by the vendors offer a level of quality and functionality that meets the needs of users throughout the campus. To determine this, the campus should undergo a requirements definition and software review process that is conducted independent of the decision process. If the institution decides that the vendor products do not meet the needs of its users, then it must decide if the vendor will be able to adequately support the institution's current products or the products of a third party that might be selected.

Legal & Ethical

From a legal perspective, administrative computing raises a set of issues different from other campus services:

■ Copyright ownership and potential violations in the use of software leased or purchased from a third party

■ Proprietary rights — who owns improvements made on a system? Who retains data and access to a system at the conclusion of the lease or licensing agreement?

■ If the campus is leasing or has purchased software, does the agreement cover improvements in the existing program? If so, at what price? Does the agreement cover system support? If so, at what price?

■ Are there needed safeguards built into the system to minimize fraud, misappropriations of funds, and other white collar crimes? Are there safeguards which minimize the ability of a single administrator to manipulate data so that a campus could be engaging in fraud when complying with a government reporting requirement?

A campus is confronted with all of these issues should it manage its own administrative computing. In addition, a campus must see to it that there are policies, procedures, or system features in place to address the following questions regardless of who operates the department:

■ Who owns system improvements developed by vendor staff, university staff, or a consultant?

■ Are their adequate safeguards concerning proprietary data about individuals to keep unauthorized persons from gaining access?

■ In terms of a campus's endowment portfolio, donor information, and the like, are there protections against abuses of insider information?

In contracting for this function, a campus must be certain that it can establish an agreement that provides the needed safeguards for all of the factors listed above as well as contract specific issues such as:

- What is the maximum down time should there be a hardware or software failure?

- Who bears the liability due to computing malfunctions (a bill that gets paid late, or a report due date being missed) that cause the campus to incur a financial penalty?

- As new technologies are developed and enhancements are made to current products, will they be supplied to the campus? At what price?

- If there are changes in FASB, GASB, or other reporting requirements which require modifications to current systems, who bears the cost of the changes?

- Will the institution continue to be eligible for educational discounts on the purchase of hardware or software?

- Does the contractor have access to a fully compatible backup system should the need arise? Who bears the cost for utilizing this system?

Administrative computing facilities have also raised a number of tax and unfair competition issues. If the facility has excess capacity which is leased to a third party by either the school or the vendor, it could create unrelated business income. Campuses have also been confronted with claims of unfair competition when they use their excess capacity to service others. If the lease of excess capacity is part of any proposed solution, the financial benefits need to be weighed against the potential public policy and public relations ramifications.

Child Care

As an emerging campus service, child care is unique among the functional areas discussed in this study. For the majority of functional areas, the decision to contract or self-operate is a choice to transition from or retain the current operating approach.

For child care, however, many institutions usually have not previously offered the service and are therefore selecting an operating approach to create as well as manage the function. While this difference in starting point may introduce requirements for child care that are not present in any of the other functions, the decision process is the same.

Financial

The key financial issue to assess is the ability of the community to pay for child care services. If the primary users of child care on a campus have a low ability to pay for the service, then the institution must decide:

- Will grants and subsidies be provided to broaden the participation in child care? At what cost?

- Who will provide those grants if child care is self-operated? If it is contract managed?

- In the absence of grants or subsidies, will enough people be able to participate to make a self-operated facility financially viable?

- Are the proposed contract managers being realistic in their estimates of participation? If they are not, what impact will that have on their revenue and cost projections?

Decision Matrix

Functional Area: Child Care

Decision Factor / Decision Process	Identify Key Participants	Develop Analytical Framework	Assess the Current Environment	Identify Customer Requirements	Develop Solution Design	Identify Solution Alternatives	Review Legal, Ethical, and Community Considerations
Financial			• Cost to provide adequate facilities	• Ability of users to pay	• Need for operations subsidies	• Need for seed money	
Human Resources				• Importance of low staff turnover	• Will students participate in staffing		• Hiring practices conform to local regulations
Mission & Culture				• Changes in composition of workforce and student body	• Will center support teacher training program		
Management Control & Efficiency			• Could a vendor with multiple sites operate center at lower cost		• What level of control does institution need to limit liability		• How to review center to enforce compliance with operating regulations
Service Quality				• Type of program needed by parents		• Employee references • Vendor track record	• Compliance with state law
Legal & Ethical Considerations					• Identify policies and procedures needed to ensure safety of children	• What risks can be transferred to a vendor	• Allegations of unfair competition

Another financial issue to consider is the cost of acquiring or renovating a facility to house the child care center and whether a vendor would be willing to share that investment. If the institution decides to contract, what costs will they still have to bear for insurance, facilities maintenance, and so on?

Human Resources

A key concern here is the ability of the institution to identify and hire qualified personnel to staff the center in a way that meets all federal and state regulations. Are there candidates for the job of center director who have experience in establishing child care programs at colleges and universities? Another issue to consider is that, given the highly personal nature of child care and the high degree of trust that is required between the center and the parent, high staff turnover is often an impediment to success. Therefore, it is important to determine whether one operating alternative provides an advantage over another in retaining the same staff for a center. Finally, the institution needs to review the potential for utilizing students to staff the center. Specifically, can students participating in teacher training programs be used to staff the center as part of their academic work? If so, will their academic department contribute to the cost of operating the center? Would a vendor be willing to allow these students to partici-pate in the operation of the center? What impact would that have on the cost of the service?

Mission & Culture

Before an institution can determine the level of financial support that it is willing to provide for a campus child care center, it needs to determine its mission. Campus child care centers are often called upon to serve many roles, including:

- Academic center to train future teachers

- Employee benefit to help attract and retain faculty and staff

- Student service to support an institution's attempt to increase enrollment by attracting older students who often have children

- A method for fostering better relations with campus employees and boosting morale and productivity.

The cost of providing child care either through self-operation or contract management needs to be weighed against the benefits that it can provide to the institution by fulfilling one or more of the missions outlined above. Some operating models lend themselves to achieving these different missions better than others. The institution needs to decide which of these missions is most important to them and then select the operating model that offers the best chance of fulfilling it.

Management Control & Efficiency

Similar to the other functions, the central questions here are whether an outside vendor would be able to operate the child care center more effectively than a self-operated center and the degree of control over the function the institution would have to relinquish. The unique question that child care introduces is whether the institution needs to maintain a greater con-trol over the policies and management of this functional area because it is dealing with the children of its students, faculty, and staff. More specifically, do the risks involved in child care (see legal section) justify sacrificing efficiency for enhanced control?

Service Quality

The need to select an operating model that will provide the highest quality of service is more important for child care than for perhaps any other campus service. The implicit trust that must be fostered between the center and its customers requires that it be able to deliver the highest level of service. Beyond the complex state regulations that mandate the quality of care and the potential liability that the campus could be exposed to, it is the very reputation of the institution that is on the line. The institution needs to carefully investigate the track record of any vendor or individual that participates in the operation of its center. Further, the institution needs to put in place a periodic review process to monitor the quality of the care that is given as well as the effectiveness of the center's educational programs. The institution should consider hiring an independent consultant familiar with child care centers to assist it in evaluating the quality of the programs being proposed and to put in place a periodic review process.

Legal & Ethical

The potential liability associated with child care is very high. This is true because the recipients of the service are children whose parents are understandably concerned about their welfare. With appropriate procedures, staff selection, and training, the risks associated with a child care program can be greatly diminished. Among the specific procedures that must be in place are:

- Developing an emergency release and medical care form

- Having the means to determine who has custody over a child and who may pick him or her up from the center

- An employee screening process to ensure that prior sex offenders are screened out

- Maintaining medical records on each child that include allergies, required medications, and present medical condition

- Utilizing the proper adult-to-child ratios and obtaining required training and certification for its staff

- Procedures for taking field trips, including parent releases, the proper type of vehicles for transportation with the proper safety features, and the like

- Protecting the confidentiality of information about the child and his or her family.

Most states now have some type of certification program for child care facilities and child care providers. All too often, these are minimum requirements which do not provide safeguards in terms of campus liability. Nevertheless, the campus needs to ensure full compliance with all applicable laws and regulations.

The campus clearly bears all the risk if it self-operates this service. It also has significant risk if it chooses to be a child care referral service. That is, if the campus program refers a parent to another service provider, the campus opens itself to risk should there be a subsequent problem. In contracting for this service the institution has three basic options:

- Have a company provide the service on-campus

- Have a company provide the service off-campus

- Provide a voucher system that can be redeemed for services off-campus.

Regardless of which of these options the institution is considering, the campus needs to identify all of the risk issues and have the vendor assume responsibility for them. Additionally, the campus needs to design an inspection process which can determine if the vendor is complying with all government and institutional standards. This is especially important if the service is being delivered off-campus.

Small business advocates view campus child care as a potential area for unfair competition. This is particularly true if the campus subsidizes the program through reduced rent or other means. Similarly, if the service is open to children other than those of students, faculty, or staff, the possibility of unfair competition allegations increases.

Finally, if the institution chooses to self-operate or contract with another non-profit organization it must make sure that any planned fund raising activities comply with all applicable state and federal regulations.

Security

Events during the past few years have underscored that campuses are not immune from the full scope of criminal activity that pervades the rest of society. This requires the institution to assemble a campus security force that can handle a wide variety of activities including:

- Enforcement of campus parking and traffic regulations

- Escort services

- Routine patrolling of campus grounds and facilities

- Response to criminal activity

- The administration and coordination of all security activities.

Some campuses have chosen to have all of these activities performed by individuals with training and certification as state police officers. At the same time, an increasing number of campuses are having functions like parking and traffic enforcement, escort services, routine patrolling, and security at special events wholly or partially performed by individuals who have not been certified as police officers. It is these activities on which the contract management/self-operation decision is focused.

Financial

In comparing the cost of self-operation to that of contract management, the institution should look at the cost of the activities that it is considering contracting for rather than the overall cost of the department. For instance, the institution could compare the per hour cost of traffic enforcement under self-operation to the cost of contracting with a vendor to provide the same service. The cost comparison should include a portion of the total costs that the institution would bear under each operating method for such centralized costs as insurance, training, overhead and administration. Then the institution can determine for each major activity that the department performs the most cost-effective way to acquire individuals with the right level of skill to ensure the campus safety. If however, the institution is considering contract management for the whole department, then the overall departmental operating costs are valid.

Decision Matrix

Functional Area: Security

Decision Factor \ Decision Process	Identify Key Participants	Develop Analytical Framework	Assess the Current Environment	Identify Customer Requirements	Develop Solution Design	Identify Solution Alternatives	Review Legal, Ethical, and Community Considerations
Financial			• Operating cost by duty				
Human Resources				• Required skills and training to safeguard campus	• Level of police versus unarmed security officers		• Impact on labor unions
Mission & Culture			• Number of campus crimes	• Relationship of police with students			
Management Control & Efficiency						• Contract entire department or selected duties	• If hybrid model – clearly delineate duties and supervising responsibility
Service Quality	• Consult with law enforcement professional			• Need for armed vs. unarmed officers••			• Training and certification of vendor's employers
Legal & Ethical Considerations	• Consult with local community police force						• Will the vendor be accountable for actions of its employees?

Human Resources

Campus security is another area where the workforce is typically unionized. As with dining services and facilities, it is necessary to be sensitive to the concerns of the union and to involve them in the decision process. It is particularly important to be responsive to the concerns of the union in the security area as any work stoppage has the potential for endangering public safety.

The other human resource-related issue that impacts the decision process in security is that of employee skill level and training. The institution must review any proposed plan carefully to ensure that each alternative utilizes individuals with the proper skills to perform the job. While using less qualified individuals may decrease costs, it exposes the campus to lawsuits, threatens its public image with students and parents, and threatens the public's safety. Here again, the institution should consider getting assistance from an independent consultant familiar with campus security operations.

Mission & Culture

The relationship between the campus community and campus security is a unique one that needs to be carefully managed. Unlike the relationship between community police and residents, campus police come in contact repeatedly with the same individuals on a daily basis. This frequent contact is a double-edged sword that can both strain and enhance the relationship between the two groups. Some professionals in the industry cite this frequent contact as being critical to enabling security forces to defuse potential confrontations with students. In deciding which of its security functions can be self-operated and which should be contracted, the institution should focus on the areas in which the activity is likely to bring the individual performing it in contact with a member of the campus community. For these activities, it must be determined:

- If the institution would benefit from having this duty performed only by individuals familiar with the campus community

- Whether these individuals can only be acquired through self-operation or whether a vendor could provide a staff that is experienced in working on a campus.

Management Control & Efficiency

In order to select the right balance of institutional control and operational efficiency, the institution needs to define its security needs. The institution needs to decide what level of security it needs to protect the campus community, safeguard its assets, maintain relations with the local community, and be responsive to the concerns of parents. The campus needs to determine the types of services it needs to provide and the corresponding level of training its staff needs to effectively perform those duties.

Service Quality

In considering contract management, the institution needs to assess the quality of the individuals that the vendor will be sending to the campus. Questions to ask the vendor include:

- What training programs and certifications do the vendor's employees have?

- Who will supervise the vendor employees while they are on the campus?

■ Can the vendor employees be held to the same standards of performance that the institution's security employees would be for performing a similar job?

■ Does the institution reserve the right to ask the vendor to remove any individual who is not performing up to the standards of quality that have been established?

Legal & Ethical

As a first step in selecting an approach to campus security, the institution needs to clearly understand the scope of permissible security activities by campus staff under state law. This will impact the institution's decision regarding under what circumstances they want security officers to be armed as well as under what circumstances security officers will have the power of arrest, both on and off campus.

If a campus wants to pursue contracting for some or all of its security requirements, it needs to be certain that the executing agreement protects the campus from a variety of liabilities. This means that the campus needs to have clarity as to the contractor's certification requirements for different tiers of employees, training programs, employee screening process, capacity to develop needed relations with law enforcement agencies, and the like. Campus officials need to fully understand the requirements of their state for campus security officers to gain access to public law enforcement data banks and investigative assistance. Similarly, campus officials should discuss the concept of utilizing contract management for all or part of their security force with local enforcement officials to determine their receptivity.

Security is an area where the campus could choose to contract-out subsets of activities (such as traffic enforcement or routine patrols) while retaining responsibility for areas like the core administration function and criminal investigations. Should a campus move in this direction, there must be clarity as to the reporting lines and demarcation of responsibility between the campus's staff and the work to be performed by the contractor(s). Since state laws on items like apprehending a suspected shoplifter and who can bear arms under what circumstances differ by jurisdiction, campus officials need to understand the requirements in their state, be certain that the contractor understands these requirements, and contractually place all liability on the contractor should the latter's employee act in violation of state laws or regulations.

Chapter IV.

Epilogue:
The Outcome of the Decision Process_____

To contract or not to contract, that is ***not*** the question. The starting point of the decision process is not to determine whether it would be better to self-operate or to contract, but to select the best operating and management approach from the array of appropriate alternatives. Focusing first on understanding how the functional area is currently operated — its strengths, weaknesses, challenges and opportunities, and the met and unmet needs of its customers — enables the institution to make a more informed choice than if its primary focus is on predicting the impact of contract management or self-operation at the outset of the process.

The structured decision process outlined in this guide is designed to assist an institution in building a set of requirements for a given functional area's operation and in identifying an appropriate set of alternatives that would meet those requirements. It is the process of comparing the campus's requirements to the characteristics of each alternative and selecting the alternative that offers the closest match that is the essence of the decision process. In addition, by encouraging the participation in the decision process of broad representation from the campus community, the institution will increase its chances for reflecting the uniqueness of the institution in its choice of operating alternative, thereby enhancing the likelihood of success.

How did the institutions presented in Chapter I resolve their contract management decisions? A summary of the outcomes of the situations presented in the case vignettes is summarized on the following pages.

Vignette #1

The vice president for facilities of a large urban university has just completed a self-assessment of his department's operations. He believes that the custodial portion of the operation is overstaffed in comparison to other institutions and industry benchmarks and that the institution is not receiving a level of service that is commensurate with the investment it is making in its custodial operations. The vice president decides to explore his options for contracting for the provision of custodial services. After seeking the input of customers, legal and union advisors, and current facilities management staff, a detailed set of specifications is developed that includes a building by building description of the level and frequency of custodial services that the university expects a vendor to provide. Bids are received from several vendors and vendor references are checked. In a presentation to the senior vice president and president, the vice president for facilities recommends that the institution accept a bid from a vendor which is offering to provide the required level and quality of services at an annual savings of $1.5 million to the institution.

The president of this institution decided to have the institution's custodial services remain self-operated. In his opinion, the potential for labor disruptions and worker vandalism that might occur as part of the union's reaction to a contract manager outweighed the benefit to the institution of lower cost and higher quality custodial services. The process did not end there, however. Working in collaboration with union leadership, the vice president for facilities was able to reduce the level of supervisory personnel, increase worker productivity, and reduce costs. In fact, the institution has almost realized all of the projected savings for the institution that were contained in the vendor proposal. The key factor here was not the operating approach that was selected but the continuous improvement process that is being collaborated on by both management and employees.

Vignette #2

The treasurer of a small suburban liberal arts college has received a proposal from the school's dining services vendor to renew its contract. The proposal offers the college significantly less revenue than the institution's current contract. This is consistent with a historical pattern that has developed at the school. A vendor offers the college a favorable initial contract that it is then unable to maintain in subsequent contracts. As a result, the college has had a series of vendors manage its dining services, with no vendor remaining beyond the initial contract. In addition, the college's students are unhappy with the quality and variety of the food and want a menu that is more tailored to the college's large contingent of vegetarians.

This liberal arts college hired an auxiliary services director with dining services experience to help it choose a new operating approach. During the course of reviewing the dining service's current operation, the new director discovered that the institution lacked the dining facilities and equipment necessary to operate efficiently. It was her contention that unless an investment was made to purchase new equipment and renovate the dining halls, it would not matter whether the institution chose self-operation or contract management as neither could be successful. The need to have greater control over managing the upgrading of the dining facilities coupled with the currently unmet customer requirements for vegetarian menu selections led the institution to elect to self-operate. The institution was able to determine that it could upgrade the facilities and alter the menu at a lower cost than any of the vendor proposals. In addition, the presence of a manager on campus with dining service experience helped tilt the scales toward self-operation at this institution.

Vignette #3

> A small suburban liberal arts college has historically contracted with a vendor to manage its campus bookstore. The current vendor's contract has just expired and although that vendor has performed satisfactorily, many members of the college's faculty and staff feel that the institution could do a better job by self-operating. The administration is concerned that the school will not be able to operate the store as cost-effectively as the vendor has. While they agree that self-operation would be more in keeping with the school's culture, they want a detailed understanding of the likely costs associated with self-operation before they agree to a change.

The management of this institution elected to self-operate its bookstore instead of renewing its contract with the current vendor. The institution decided that it could be at least as successful financially as it had been under contract management and that the potential for exceeding the revenue it had received from the contractor outweighed the risk of operating losses that it would now have to bear. As a further benefit, the college felt that a self-operated store would be able to carry many of the academic tradebooks that the faculty wanted sold in the store but that the vendor was unwilling to stock. The decision was recommended to the administration by a committee of students, faculty, and staff who worked with an experienced bookstore manager from a local school (who was admittedly biased toward self-operation) to identify the likely costs and complexities of self-operation. While the store is only in its first year of self-operation, all results to date have been positive. In fact, the institution has seen a boost in the morale of employees, both within the bookstore and in other functional areas, who view the switch as a vote of confidence by the college in the abilities of its employees.

Vignette #4

> A new senior management team has been put in place at a large urban university. As one of the outcomes of its assessment of the university's current financial and operational condition, a decision was made to upgrade the institution's information systems. Senior management is not confident that the current administrative computing leadership has the capabilities to perform a complicated multi-year systems implementation. Further, it is their assessment that the university has not been receiving an acceptable level of return on its investment in technology.

After assessing the capabilities of its in-house management team, this institution determined that the most cost-effective way to upgrade the university's administrative information systems was to employ a contractor to operate the administrative computing function. The institution selected a vendor that would manage the administrative computing operation as well as implement new systems and technologies that would be consistent with its technology strategy. The institution was able to reach an agreement with the vendor to offer employment to all of its current staff and to match their current compensation packages. While this requirement did raise the cost of the vendor's services, the institution felt it was an important consideration that justified the investment. The university cited a better return on investment offered by the vendor and the transfer of the risks of the implementation to the vendor as the primary factors in their decision.

Vignette #5

> The long-time director of physical plant for a small liberal arts college has suffered a heart attack that causes him to choose early retirement. The current assistant director is relatively inexperienced and is not prepared to take on the director's job. The college's treasurer is faced with the choice of conducting a search for a new director or contracting with a vendor to manage the department. Further compounding the decision is a recent report from a facilities consulting firm that concluded that the facilities department was not operating efficiently and needed to upgrade and modernize its procedures and the level of knowledge of its workforce. The college has recently completed construction of a new science center and the board of trustees is not confident that the current facilities department has the skills to maintain its more complex systems. Historically, the facilities department has required a disproportionate amount of the treasurer's time, and she wants the new management team to be able to run the department without as much day-to-day direction from her.

This institution chose a hybrid approach to operating its facilities. Instead of continuing to self-operate or to contract for the operation of its facilities department, it hired a vendor to manage the department. The vendor is in effect acting as director of physical plant, while all of the physical plant staff remain employees of the college. The college felt that this hybrid approach most closely met its needs for an experienced director to introduce sound processes and training programs to improve the quality and productivity of the department staff, while eliminating the need for the treasurer to participate in the day-to-day management of the department. By employing a contractor, the institution also gained access to the expertise of the vendor in energy management, computer systems and other advanced building systems that it could not afford to have on staff on a full-time basis.

★★★★★

The ultimate choice of operating method for a functional area will be unique to each specific campus and function. One institution's success with a particular form of self-operation or contract management is not automatically transferable to another. It is not sufficient for a campus decision maker to choose to operate the way ABC College operates. Each campus has its own unique set of requirements, culture, and community that need to drive its selection of an operating model. However, institutions can take the same approach to identify and interpret these unique characteristics regardless of the function or service. To be successful, the decision process needs to:

■ Objectively assess each alternative

■ Employ a methodology that will withstand close scrutiny

■ Encourage broad participation from the campus community

■ Consider the broad array of factors that impact the choice of operating model

■ Build a consensus for the preferred operating approach.

The institutions discussed above elected to utilize different approaches to operating different campus functions, but they nonetheless have one thing in common. The ultimate success of their operations will not depend on whether they chose to contract for part or all of their services or whether they chose to self-operate. Success is driven not by the operating philosophy, but rather by the quality of the management team, its responsiveness to the needs of the campus, and the effectiveness of the partnership between the functional area's managers, its customers and the campus administration. It is for these reasons that a *structured decision process* such as the one outlined in this guide is so important. Selecting self-operation over contract management, or vice versa, without due consideration of the array of factors that will ultimately impact the operation is unlikely to lead to long-term success. This guide, therefore, while it will not make the decision for an institution, does outline a process that supports informed and effective decision making.

Appendices

Appendix A: The Contract

The drafting of a contract presents a host of legal questions. Many of them can be resolved through relatively standard "boilerplate" sections. In this category are issues on insurance, choice of law, amendments to the agreement, and the like. Please see Exhibit 1 for a sample set of such clauses.

Exhibit 1 also contains sample clauses for many of the other common provisions in contracts for a campus service. Among the provisions addressed in Exhibit 1 are those sections on financial terms, facility improvements, and the contract term (length of the agreement). These types of sections need to be written to cover the specific facts and circumstances surrounding the institution and the service to be let. As with all contract terms, a goal in these sections is that the writing be clear and specific to avoid disagreements as to interpretation. For instance, if the campus wants the ability to terminate the contract without cause, then this should be so stated. But the campus must recognize that clauses of this nature are normally two-sided. That is, if the campus has this right so will the contractor. Such a clause has worked to the advantage of the campus when it has a desire to change contractors prior to the conclusion of the full contract term, but the contractor has not engaged in such egregious behavior as to have cause for termination. Key to the campus's ability to exercise this clause is having a turnover plan in place. A second important element is timing. It is much easier to change operators during the summer than it is in the middle of the school year. On the other hand, contractors have used this type of clause to their advantage by giving notice to terminate services at a difficult time for the institution. This has most often occurred where the time period for notice is relatively short (30 days) and the contractor knows that the campus is not prepared to assume this responsibility.

Similar problems occur in contracts with a "buy-out clause." One reason why campuses often contract a service is to have a third party invest in facilities, equipment, operating systems, and furnishings for which the campus lacks funds. Typically the contractor will recover its principle and interest using a straightline form of depreciation. Thus, if the contractor is to invest $100,000 and the contract term is five years, the contractor will show a $20,000 per year expense plus appropriate interest. If the contract is terminated prior to five years, typically the campus must pay the contractor for the unamortized portion. If the dollar amount of this debt is significant in comparison to the value of the contracted service, this puts the campus at a disadvantage should it want to contract with another vendor or assume operation itself. In the former case, all other vendors will underscore the front-end cost that they must incur, and they will normally take the position that the "improvements" that are now being acquired are valueless.

Campuses which are cash poor, have a good grasp as to the value of the improvements that the contractor is making, and who gain improvements to both the infrastructure as well as those elements which are visible to the customer, often find this to be a reasonable risk. A second key element is to be certain that the improvements to be gained through this investment will carry the campus through the contract term. If the campus is contracting for custodial services, with a major investment by the contractor in cleaning equipment, it is important that the equipment be usable in the last years of the contract. Otherwise the campus faces the situation where its choice is to have the contractor invest more, normally on the agreement to extend the contract term, or to have sub-par service because of defective equipment.

One campus entering into a multi-year food service agreement did not want to have the obligation of a buy-out clause. This campus negotiated an investment package which had the contractor paying for facility renovations, new equipment and furniture on an annual basis. Each year the contractor took as an expense that year's investment. This campus avoided the potential difficulty of a large cash payment to cancel the agreement, while also assuring itself of significant annual improvement in its food service facilities. As can be seen, legal issues and the transfer of risk merge operational and financial issues, with matters of law and policy issues.

The privileges and responsibilities of the parties make up a third critical set of contract sections. In these sections the campus wants to be certain that campus policies are followed, that the contractor will comply with all applicable rules and regulations and that there is clarity as to where the contractors responsibilities and scope of services begin and end. It is critical that the campus retain all of the privileges and management oversight responsibility that it may want to exercise in these sections. Anything that the campus does not specifically retain will reasonably be assumed by the contractor to be forfeited.

This is also where the detail of the contractor's responsibilities is included. In contracts for services like the college store and food service, the contractor is particularly concerned about the scope of its "exclusive rights" to specified services. It is the goal of the contractor to gain as broad a scope as possible. Campuses need to protect sales by student organizations and other support groups, the opportunity to provide services by other campus departments or contractors, and for new, not yet identified, ventures in the future. As with most sections of the contract, for the campus to represent itself well it must have thought through issues like these and have a clear negotiating position.

All of the commentators on contracting agree the monitoring of contract compliance is essential. To accomplish this, campuses might want to include the requirement of periodic management and financial audits. The latter could be done either by an independent auditor (if so, have it built into the contractor's expenses) and/or the institution's own staff. Of equal importance is the requirement of periodic audits as to the contractor's compliance with the agreement's service requirements and campus regulations. To accomplish these types of management audits, the campus must clearly delineate a set of measurable service objectives and the specific campus regulations with which the contractor must comply.

Exhibit 2 enumerates many of the sections which the typical contract should include. The reader must understand that campus policies and state and federal laws and regulations may mandate certain requirements for a contract of this nature. It should also be recognized that the services which are being let, as well as the size of the services, will impact the length and complexity of the contract.

Recognizing the increasing scrutiny by legislators and government officials of the non-profit community, it is essential that in all facets of the contracting process the behavior of campus officials be totally ethical. This means not only full compliance with the letter of state law and campus policies, but with the spirit with which these laws and policies were implemented. Campuses should have very clear policies on the acceptance of any type of gratuities from its contractors and potential contractors. Campuses should also have clearly enunciated policies on communications with all vendors that assure equal access and treatment.

Allegations of favoritism in the letting of a contract can have a terrible impact on the campus's public image. The negative impact can occur even when the campus can show that it has acted properly. From the perspective of the accusing party and the media, the issue is often not whether an actual impropriety occurred, but whether from the facts and circumstances one can reasonably believe that it may have occurred. One campus in the Midwest has been confronted with allegations of impropriety in the letting of a service for over a year. Charges, counter-charges, denials, and the like have been carried in campus and local media on an ongoing basis. Irrespective of the accuracy of the media coverage, both the campus and the vendor have been harmed.

EXHIBIT 1

Sample Contract Sections

Notes:

1. The term "Campus" refers to the college, university, or foundation contracting for a given service.

2. Some other provisions which follow will need to be modified depending on the nature of the service(s) being contracted. For instance, if the agreement is to cover custodial services (or another cost center), the Financial Provisions will address payments due from the Campus to the Contractor.

3. Consultation with the institution's local attorney is essential to be certain that the Campus is following the laws and regulations operable to it.

Contract Term Provisions

Contract Term. This agreement shall commence on (month/day/year) and terminate on (month/day/year).

Contract Modification. The parties may modify this agreement in writing only, signed by their respective authorized representatives.

Termination for Cause. Should there be a material breech of contract or Contractor fail to substantially perform Campus may put contractor on written notice that such defect must be corrected within thirty (30) calendar days. Should Contractor fail to remedy a defect, breech, or failure to perform within the stated period, the Contractor shall be given sixty (60) calendar days written notice of cancellation. Should there be disagreement amongst the parties on this matter it shall be submitted to binding arbitration.

Termination/Suspension of the Contract — Immediate. Should there be a material breech of the contract which puts at risk the Contractor's ability to perform (e.g., refusal by vendors to deliver goods due to non-payment of bills; repeated and/or gross violations of health and safety codes), or if the Contractor is not providing a service per the contract which is required for normal operation of the Campus (e.g., non-service of meals in a board program; refusal to order required course material), Campus may take whatever steps are necessary to see to the immediate provision of the needed service. This may include immediate cancellation of the contract, suspension of all or part of the contract, and/or other actions in order to meet this immediate need.

Termination by Choice. Either party may terminate this agreement for any reason upon 120 days written notice to the other party.

Contract Renewal. The Campus may, at its sole discretion, extend this agreement on the same terms and conditions for a period not to exceed ___ years after the contract term as defined in section ____.

Annual Contract Review. Should aggregate student enrollment (measured by headcount) for any single academic year be plus or minus __%, the parties agree to reevaluate the financial terms as specified in Sec. _____ and _____ , as well as the operation of impacted specifics. Furthermore, should Contractors total financial return (measured as the total of General & Administrative Expense plus Net Income) exceed an aggregate of __% for any two-year period, the parties agree to reevaluate the financial terms, the scope of services, and pricing to the customer.

Campus Rights and Privileges Provisions

Campus Approval of Subcontractors. Contractor shall obtain written consent from Campus prior to contracting with a Subcontractor and any such contract shall be subject to the terms and conditions prescribed by Campus, if any. In requesting said approval, Contractor shall append the proposed agreement between it and its Subcontractor. Contractor is fully responsible for all actions of it subcontractors and shall assure that its subcontractors, if any, fulfill all obligations and responsibilities enumerated in this agreement.

Proprietary Rights. All proprietary information disclosed by Campus to Contractor shall be held in confidence and shall be used only in the performance of this agreement. Campus shall own all documents regarding textbook orders and sales, pricing, inventory, and sale by merchandising category in the University Student Store, as well as in all other service units operated by Contractor. Contractor does not forfeit its proprietary interest in trademark or copyright products or operating systems by virtue of this agreement. Nevertheless, Contractor agrees to give all operating systems used by Contractor in providing the services covered by this agreement to the Campus at the termination of this agreement. Unless specified else-where in this agreement, said systems shall be given to Campus at no cost. The sole exception to this requirement is software limited by suppliers' licensing agreements. Contractor must advise the Campus of all software for which said agreements are in place.

Access to Facilities. Contractor shall permit the Contract Administrator or other Campus-authorized representatives to inspect any and all areas of (list specific areas) and other areas under its control during normal operating hours, and at any time in the event of an emergency. Campus reserves the right to enter (list of specific areas) and other Contractor service areas for inspections, repairs, alterations, or additions hereto or other portions of the building in which these and other services provided by the Contractor are located during regular business hours unless an emergency exists.

Product Limitations Due to Campus Policy. The contractor will be willing to refrain from the display or sale of any item requested by the Campus. Such requests shall not be made arbitrarily or capriciously. It shall only be made as to lines or types of goods, not as to specific manufacturers or brands.

Waiver of Rights. Any delay or failure to enforce any provision of this agreement shall not constitute a waiver or limitations of Campus's rights under this agreement.

Contractor's Responsibilities Provisions

Independent Contractor. The Contractor is an independent contractor, not an employee or partner, of the Campus. Contractor's acts or representations with respect to third parties are not binding upon the Campus.

Return of all Campus Furniture and Fixtures. At the termination of this agreement, Contractor will return all Campus provided furniture and fixtures in the same condition as when provided, except for normal wear and tear. The parties will prepare a list of such furniture and fixtures and append it to this agreement within sixty (60) days from the effective date of this agreement. Additions and deletions will be noted annually.

Damage to Inventory or Other Property. Contractor assumes the risk of loss or damage to inventory or other property while in transit to or from the Campus, while on the Campus, or while in the areas leased to the Contractor by the Campus. Such risk of loss includes, but is not limited to, loss of money, checks, and credit card collections or theft of inventory or other property.

Key Control. Contractor shall pay a nominal, refundable deposit and shall be responsible for the control of keys issued by the Campus and the security of those areas provided for Contractor's use. The Campus shall be responsible for the costs of rekeying and replacing lock cylinders when the Campus initiates such activity. Contractor shall be responsible for the costs of key replacement, rekeying, or lock replacement when the Contractor's negligence requires such work.

General Indemnity Clause. It is the intent of the parties that Contractor shall bear all costs associated with its responsibilities under the contract. In addition to any costs already enumerated, this shall include all penalties and fines for violation of applicable government regulations and laws, as well as the cost of correcting any such violations. Similarly, Contractor shall indemnify and hold harmless the Campus, the System (if applicable), and their agents, governing board, officers, directors, employees, etc., for any acts by the Contractor, its agents, employees, etc., which may cause injury or damage to persons or property. Said indemnification shall cover not only the cost of the actual damages, but any other costs attendant thereto (e.g., attorney fees, court costs).

Public and Product Liability Insurance/Indemnity Clause. Contractor shall maintain public liability and product liability insurance (comprehensive general liability coverage), at its expense, with a qualified company who can do business in the State of _____ of not less than ___ million and 00/100s ($_,000,000) dollars combined single limit. Said policy shall cover all facets of the Lessee's operation in conjunction with the Campus. The policy shall contain a covenant by the company issuing same, that the policy shall not be cancelled by the issuing company for any reason unless a thirty (30) day written notice of cancellation first be provided to the Campus and the (System office, if applicable). The policy shall name as additional insureds, (list all other desired parties, e.g., the Trustees of _____), and their agents, officers, directors, and employees. Certificates of the policy or policies representing the same shall be delivered to the Campus annually and retained by it. All premiums on said policy shall be paid by the Contractor.

Insurance for All Furniture, Fixtures, and the Like. Contractor shall maintain, for the term of this agreement and any renewal thereof, insurance insuring all of the furniture, fixtures, equipment, and inventory located in or upon the (list all areas under contractor's control) and other areas used by the Contractor against casualty losses caused by earthquake, fire, vandalism, snow, flood, lightening, windstorm, hail, explosion, riot, civil commotion, aircraft, vehicle, smoke, or other casualties which the Campus might designate. Such insurance shall be for an amount not less that the replacement cost of the covered items. Contractor shall purchase such insurance from a company authorized to do business in the State of _____, and Contractor shall provide the Campus with certificates evidencing proof of such insurance.

Liability Insurance. The Contractor shall maintain, for the term of this agreement and any renewals thereof, public liability, product liability, and all other insurance as is normally carried in like settings or as specified elsewhere in this agreement.

Performance Bond. The Contractor shall maintain to the Campus's benefit a letter of credit or payment bond, renewable each year at the option of the campus, in the amount of one year's guaranteed minimum income. Should the Contractor elect to furnish and maintain a payment bond, the bond shall be executed by a corporate surety authorized to do business in (State), executed on forms approved by the Attorney General of (State).

Payment of All Taxes, Licenses, and Fees. Contractor shall pay all taxes and all license and permit fees now in existence or which may be incurred due to this agreement or the services provided hereunder. Contractor shall be responsible for complying with any applicable federal, state and local laws, codes and regulations, in connection with any and all services covered by this agreement.

Compliance with All Laws, Regulations, and Policies. Contractor shall comply with all Campus policies and federal and state laws, rules, and regulations concerning nondiscrimination in employment.

Environmental Health and Safety. Contractor shall, at its direct cost, comply fully with all applicable federal and state laws, rules, and regulations concerning environmental health and safety. Contractor shall permit inspections of all service units under its control by the Campus's safety officers, and Contractor shall comply in a timely manner with all directives issued by the Campus concerning environmental health and safety.

Labor Relations. Contractor shall be solely responsible for its own labor relations with any trade or union representative and shall negotiate and adjust all disputes between itself and its employees or any union representing its employees. Contractor shall comply fully with all applicable federal and state laws, rules, and regulations concerning employment and labor relations.

Whenever the Contractor has knowledge that any actual or potential labor dispute is delaying or threatens to delay the timely performance of work under the contract, the Contractor shall immediately give notice thereof including all relevant information with respect to the Contract Administrator and/or his or her designated representative.

Contractor Use of Campus Property. The Campus shall retain title to all property which they either furnish to the Contractor upon the commencement of this Agreement or any time thereafter. Contractor shall use such property only in the performance of this Agreement unless the Contract Administrator authorizes otherwise in writing. Contractor shall not use or remove any other property which it purchases for use (list locations) or elsewhere on the Campus without the prior written approval of the Contract Administrator.

Security. The Campus shall provide the (list sites managed by Contractor, e.g., University Student Store, Food Service) with general police security in accordance with similar Campus security procedures elsewhere on the (name of) campus. The Campus will provide any additional security which the Contractor requires at the Contractor's sole cost and expense at rates customary for such services. The Contractor shall not employ its own security staff without approval of the Campus. Contractor shall comply with Campus policies concerning criminal or other improper conduct, and Contractor shall report all such incidents to the Contract Administrator. Except when an emergency condition requires otherwise, contractor shall summon the Campus Police Department for all public emergency situations.

Compliance with Campus Security Procedures. The Contractor and its employees shall comply with all Campus rules and regulations governing access, key control, and conduct on Campus property. Campus agrees to furnish Contractors' personnel with identification required for entrance to or exit from Campus premises during normal work hours. It shall be the responsibility of the Contractor to return any and all identification to the Campus within one (1) day of personnel no longer employed at the Campus premises or for employees removed from the premises at the request of the Contract Administrator.

Liens. Contractor shall keep the Campus free and clear from all liens asserted by any person or firm for any reason arising out of the furnishing of services or materials by or to Contractor.

Contractor Representations in its Response to the RFP. Contractor shall fulfill all commitments desired by the Campus made in its response to the RFP, even if particular commitments are not specifically addressed in this agreement.

Exclusive Rights (College Store). The vendor shall have the exclusive right to sell traditional college bookstore products. The sole exception to this are sales permitted by Campus policy by officially recognized student organizations. The purpose of said sales by student organizations is to raise funds for their cultural, recreational, and community service programs. Campus policy limits such sales to specified campus locations, a limited number of sales days per month for a single organization and that the goods to be sold shall not be commercially manufactured unless said goods are directly related to the organizations purpose (e.g., an environmental organization selling Sierra Club calendars). Exceptions to this exclusion will require the written prior approval of the Contractor and shall be presented to the Contractor only by the Contract Administrator. (Note: this clause should be modified based on the services being contracted.)

Payment of All Operating Expenses. All direct operating expenses such as labor, acquisition of goods for resale, operating supplies, advertising and promotions, shipping, telephone, and postage are the sole responsibility of the Contractor.

Medical Requirements (of particular importance in food service and child care). Contractor shall insure that all of its employees assigned to work on the Campus meet all applicable medical requirements of all government entities prior to the commencement of work and shall adhere to any and all federal, state, local, and Campus guidelines and regulations.

FINANCIAL PROVISIONS

Annual Guarantee. Not withstanding any provision on this Agreement to the Contrary, Contractor shall pay the Campus a Minimum Guarantee in the following amounts during the years of the contract terms as indicated:

, 199_ to   , 199_: $_____

, 199_ to   , 199_: $_____ ... etc.

Percentage of Sales. In each calendar year of operation, Contractor shall determine a Percentage Amount based upon the following formula:

_% of all Sales from the (List all appropriate units) (Note: this % often increases based upon total sales FTE, or some similar measurement.)

In this section, "Sales" means gross sales, exclusive of computer hardware/software sales, sales at the agreed-to discount for purchases by the Campus and other University auxiliaries, less refunds, voids, and local taxes. In each of the years described in section _____ above, if the Percentage Amount exceeds the Minimum Guarantee for that year, Contractor shall pay the Campus the Percentage Amount. In no event shall Contractor pay the Campus less than the Minimum Guarantee for the applicable year of the contract term.

Payment Upon Early Termination. In the event either the Contractor or the Campus terminates this Agreement as provided above, Contractor shall pay the Campus the percentage of all Sales in place for that year up to the date of termination.

Financial Record and Reports. Contractor agrees to the following reporting and recording requirements at its direct cost:

1. Contractor shall maintain complete and accurate records of all transactions in accordance with accepted industry standards and shall keep such records for a period of not less than five years after the termination of this agreement. Contractor shall make available for inspection by the Campus during normal business hours all records which the Contractor makes in the course of performing its obligations under this agreement.

2. Contractor shall maintain substantiating accounting records, including but not limited to gross sales, refunds, net discount sales by category, cash receipts and deposits, inventory purchases, accounts payable, accounts receivable, payroll and personnel records, and payments due to the Campus. Contractor will meet with the Contract Administrator upon request to review each period statement. Campus shall have the right to require an annual independent audit of contractor's sales and commission payments under this agreement at Contractor's expense.

3. Contractor shall furnish Campus with monthly sales reports and quarterly profit and loss statements. Contractor will meet with the Contract Administrator upon request to review such statements. Contractor will reflect on the next period's statement all adjustments required by any review and audit.

4. Contractor shall provide the Campus with an audited financial statement for the Contractor's corporation within three months after the end of each of the Contractor's fiscal year during the contract term of this agreement.

5. During (month) of each contract year during this agreement, Contractor shall provide the Campus with an annual and monthly projection of sales by classification for the coming fiscal year.

Payment Terms. The Contractor shall make the payments required by this agreement in accordance with the following:

1. Contractor shall pay the Campus on a semi–annual basis. On the first business day of every second quarter, Contractor shall pay the Campus one-half of the Minimum Guarantee. If the Contractor determines that it owes the Campus a greater payment as required by section _____, it shall pay the balance of such amount not later than __ days after the end of the applicable quarter.

2. If Contractor fails to make any payment within ten days after the required payment date, Contractor shall pay, in addition to any other amounts due, a late charge of ___% per annum of the amount due and a nonrefundable processing charge of $___ per late payment.

3. Contractor shall deliver all payments to the (office, room number, building name) or mailed to the following address:

   (Office name)
   (Name of University)
   (Street Address)
   (City, State, Zip Code)

4. Contractor also agrees to advance up to the first _____ years of the annual minimum guarantee upon execution of this document and continue to advance up to three years during the term of this agreement. Campus may choose to exercise this clause at any time.

Non-Competition. Contractor agrees not to operate (list the services) or other business in competition with campus-owned services covered by this agreement, regardless of whether the Campus operates such service itself or contracts its operation, for a period of one (1) year following termination of this agreement or any renewal of this agreement.

Facility Improvements. Contractor shall fund improvements of the (list areas/buildings) at an amount of not less than $_____ nor more than $_____ without offset or amortization of amounts payable under this agreement. These renovations shall include structural changes to the building, changes to mechanical or electrical systems, permanently installed floor coverings or wall coverings, and other work which the Campus might approve. These funds will also be used to acquire operating equipment, fixtures, and systems as agreed to by the parties. In advance of contracting for such renovations or otherwise commencing work, contractor shall fully describe the nature of contemplated renovations and provide a written estimate of their costs. The Contract Administrator shall approve all renovations in advance. Contractor shall present items of renovation costs to the Contract Administrator in the same manner as estimates. Contractor shall complete all renovations required by this agreement no later than (month/date/year).

Purchase of Inventory Held for Resale. Upon the termination of this agreement or any renewal thereof, the Campus may repurchase inventory from the contractor as specified in Appendix _.

GENERAL PROVISIONS

Notice. Any notice required by this agreement shall be deemed given when made in writing and personally delivered by courier, deposited with the United States Postal Service by certified or registered mail, return receipt requested, or by facsimile transmission addressed as follows:

TO CAMPUS:
   (Person's Name)
   (Title of Position)
   (Name of Campus)
   (Name of University)
   (Street Address)
   (City, State, Zip Code)

WITH COPIES TO:
    (Name of Person)
    (Title of Position)
    (Name of University)
    (Street Address)
    (City, State, Zip Code)

    (Name of Person)
    (Title of Position)
    (Name of University)
    (Street Address)
    (City, State, Zip Code)

TO CONTRACTOR:
    (Name of Person)
    (Title of Position)
    (Name of Company)
    (Street Address)
    (City, State, Zip Code)

WITH COPY TO:
    (Name of Person)
    (Title of Position)
    (Name of Company)
    (Street Address)
    (City, State, Zip Code)

Binding of Successors. This agreement shall inure to the benefit and shall be binding upon the legal representatives, successors-in-interest, and assigns of the parties hereto.

Sole Agreement. This document constitutes the sole agreement of the parties on the subject matter hereof, and any prior understandings or agreements, written or oral, are of no effect. This agreement may not be amended or modified except in writing signed by all parties hereto.

All appendices referenced in this agreement, whether or not attached hereto, are incorporated herein for all purposes.

Assignment. Except as provided elsewhere in this agreement, this agreement may not be assigned by either party, hereto except upon the written approval of the other party.

Severability. Each provision of this agreement is severable, and if any provision is held to be invalid or unenforceable, the remainder of the provisions shall remain in effect.

Choice of Law and Venue. This agreement shall be construed under the laws of the State of (where Campus is located); venue in any action to enforce this agreement shall be in _____ County, (State).

Force Majeure. Neither party shall be responsible for losses resulting from the failure to perform any terms or provisions of this agreement if the failure is attributable to a natural phenomenon, fire, disorder, or other condition beyond the reasonable control of the party whose performance is impaired thereby, and which, by the exercise of reasonable diligence, such party is unable to prevent, provided however, that monies payable at the time of such circumstances shall be payable as required by this agreement.

Suspension of Service. The obligation of either party to perform any acts herein specified shall be suspended during the periods such performance is prevented by act of God, war, riot, invasion, fire, accident, government interference, regulations, appropriations, rationing or by priority, inability to secure goods, materials, shipments, or any other occurrence beyond the control of the Contractor. It is expected, however, that the Contractor will make a good-faith effort to provide some service during the most difficult times (hurricanes, for example). In the event that Contractor is unable to provide a service for any of the reasons specified, Campus is authorized to provide such service in such a manner as it may deem appropriate and to use any food or supplies of Contractor which are available provided that Campus shall reimburse the Contractor for such supplies actually used at Contractor's actual cost. This, however, does not relieve the Contractor from the responsibility of serving Campus if the Contractor's employees go on strike.

Termination of Contract. The Contractor shall restore all facilities under its control to the Campus upon the effective date of termination along with all facilities, equipment, and other items furnished by the Campus or purchased for use under the terms of this agreement, in the condition which it was received, reasonable wear and tear excepted. The Contractor shall be responsible for all losses and damages to the (units managed by Contractor) and other facilities used by the Contractor, resulting from its default or failure.

Wage and Price Control. The Contractor warrants that it is in complete compliance with all laws, rules, regulations, and orders of the federal, state, and local governments and any department, agency, or commission thereof empowered to effect a plan of wage or price control. Further, the Contractor warrants that the amount invoiced under the contract will not exceed the limit of (A) the contract price or (B) the maximum levels established in accordance with the above. This shall also pertain to all subcontracts issued under the contract.

EXHIBIT 2

Contract Sections

The outline which follows covers most of the factors required in any auxiliary service contract. Items may be added or deleted according to the specific service being contracted, the needs and policies of the institution, and state law.

* Preamble....Name of the agreement and an introductory statement naming the parties.

1. The Purpose....States why the parties are entering into the agreement.

2. The Work....Notes what is being contracted for, often specifying service sites, initial hours of operation and other similar items.

3. Term and Termination

   A. Contract Term. Beginning and ending dates.

   B. Contract Modification. How the parties can change the contract.

   C. Contract Termination. How the agreement may be ended prior to the ending date specified in Section III–A.

4. Rights and Obligations of the College/University

   A. Contract Administrator. Name by position the key institutional liaison.

   B. University Obligations. Enumerate all tasks the institution will perform and all its commitments. These could include custodial or maintenance responsibilities retained by the institution, allowing the contractor's employees to have privileges normally give to institution employees only (i.e., parking permits) allowing the contractor to use the institution's telephone system or mailroom, access to certain institutional equipment, and access to institutional operating systems.

   C. Institutional Rights. Enumerate actions by the contractor which require prior approval by the institution. Each major item usually has a separate section. Typical items include:

      1. Approval of all prices.

      2. Approval of all subcontractors.

      3. Approval for the appointment.

      4. Approval of new service lines, discontinuance of major service lines, menu review, etc.

      5. Alteration in service sites or hours.

      6. Any modification of facilities and any major equipment acquisition.

      7. Approval of uniform, signage, and advertising.

   D. Delinquent Accounts. State any institutional responsibility for the collection of unpaid bills.

E.   Key Control. Normally the institution wants to maintain control of the cutting of all keys and lock cores. This section specifies how the contractor may request keys and the level of the key distribution the institution will allow.

F.   Proprietary Rights. Certain items and systems the institution owns and shares with the contractor while retaining the right of disclosure to any other party, and vice versa.

G.   Institutional Indemnity. How the institution will protect the contractor from the acts of its employees and those under its control.

H.   Rights Retained. Any future action the institution wants to control (e.g., in contracting the bookstore, the institution may want to retain the right to a service which a bookstore might want to offer).

I.   Special Section(s). Unique items to which the parties may agree to (e.g., in contracting the bookstore, the institution may want to retain the right to a service which a bookstore might want to offer).

J.   Waiver of Rights. States that if the institution does not exercise a specific right, it does not forfeit that right, then states under what circumstances the institution can forfeit a right.

5.   Rights and Obligations of the Contractor

A.   Contractor's Obligations. A detailed list of what the contractor will do. This includes the goods/services the contractor will provide, pricing policy, menus, textbook ordering policy, preventive maintenance schedule, cleaning schedule, refund policy, frequency of equipment replacement, and all other items the contractor must do. Use one or more appendices for detailed information.

B.   Operating Budget. A detailed list of revenues and expenditures per the institution's specifications. In some cases the contractor may not incur certain expenditures without the authorization of the institution.

C.   Facility and Equipment Audit. The contractor's obligation to maintain certain facilities and equipment at an agreed-to level. Should also specify periodic joint audits by the institution and contractor.

D.   Program Audit. Institution to assure the contractor's compliance with the terms of the contract.

E.   Financial Audit. A list of the contractor's financial information that will be available to the institution. Dictates which financial records must be maintained on the campus.

Note: Many institutions garner much of this information through the requirement of a monthly report.

F.   Sanitation and Safety. Includes standards the contractor agrees to maintain, as well as the institution's right to inspect sites.

G.   Staff Supervision. The commitment of the contractor to have adequate staff supervision on site. Also clearly states that the institution will not exercise any supervisory control over any employee of the contractor, but that the contract administrator is available for consultation.

H.   Labor Issues. Determines the contractor's obligation to those employed by the institution or the former contractor to perform this service immediately prior to this contract, the contractor's relationship with its own employees, the contractor's responsibility to inform the institution of any impending labor dispute, appropriate equal opportunity and affirmative action statements, and the rights of either party to hire the other's employees.

I. Contractors Use of Institution-Owned Property. Specifies where and why the contractor may use times belonging to the institution.

J. Security Issues. States the institution's right of access to areas under the contractor's control, the rights of the institutional police and the extent to which the contractor must abide by the institution's approach to disciplinary actions.

K. Assignment of Rights. Conditions under which the contractor may give or sell a right or obligation covered by the contract.

L. Cooperation with all Departments and Other Contractors. States the required behavior of the contractor toward other entities on the campus.

M. Insurance. Sets out the minimum monetary levels of all insurance the contractor must provide. Requires the contractor to provide the institution with a certificate of insurance covering the institution, all institutional employees, all members of the governing board, the state, and any other individuals or entities the institution wants covered. The certificate should contain a statement that it cannot be canceled or altered without the institution receiving notice within a specified period of time.

N. Contractor Indemnity. States how the contractor will protect the institution for its acts, the acts of its employees and agents and all other parties under its control.

O. Special Sections: Unique obligations the contractor agrees to perform, such as responding to customer input, marketing program, or debit card.

P. Performance Bond or Letter of Credit. Guarantees the institution will receive some predetermined compensation if the contractor defaults.

6. Financial Arrangements

A. The Fee. Payment of either a flat amount, a percentage of the net or gross income, a division of profits/savings, or any other means or combination.

B. Payment Terms. The timing, place, and means of the payment terms.

C. Investment Package. Any obligation to invest in facilities, equipment and fixtures. States the amount of the investment, the decision-making process and the payment terms. This section also includes any buy-out requirement.

D. Contractor Payments for Facility Improvements Prior to Assuming Management of the Account. May be included if the contractor is committed to paying for an investment package that had occurred under prior management.

E. Payments by the Institution to the Contractor. Covers the amount, timing, and means for all payments by the institution to the contractor, including board fees collected by the institution, debit card expenses when deposits are held by the institution, and fees for services provided to the institution.

F. Bad Debts. Determines who bears responsibility for the collection of and nonpayment of account receivable.

G. Contractor Expenses. Lists the type of expense the contractor may charge against the account. This section states permissibility and level of management fee for the contracting company.

H. Purchase of Inventory. States the contractor's right or obligation to purchase the inventory of items for sale, raw food products and consumable supplies, and the terms for such purchase. Also states the right or obligation of the institution or subsequent contractor to repurchase these items.

7. Miscellaneous Provisions

 A. Suspension of Services. Under what circumstances (e.g., natural disaster, student riot, labor unrest) either party may be relieved of any obligations.

 B. Wage and Price Controls. The impact of federal or state legislation of this nature.

 C. Choice of Law. In interpreting the contract or any legal action arising from the contract, this provision specifies which state's laws will apply. This section may also include a statement as to where the parties agree to engage in any litigation. Most states require all publicly funded schools to specify that litigation shall occur within the state.

 D. Provisions Separable. Allows all other section of the contract to stand if a court determines a particular section is unenforceable.

 E. Force Majeure. States that neither party is responsible for acts beyond its control and under what circumstances the party will be freed from specific obligations.

 F. Amendments. Specifies the process by which the contract may be changed.

 G. Notice. How and to whom any official notice must be delivered.

 H. Sole Agreement. States that this document, all specified appendices, and all appropriate amendments or modifications as allowed in the body of the writing are the entire agreement between the parties. No other writing or communication can in any way alter the contract.

 I. Exclusivity. The extent to which the contractor is granted the sole right to anything on the campus and to which locales this right extends.

 J. Non-Competition. The agreement of the parties not to engage in a similar service or to allow a similar service in its facilities within a given area.

 K. Binding on Successors. Commits to fulfill the agreement with those whom, for any reason, assume the role of one of the parties.

* Signature Provision – The place for signing of the contract by the person(s) authorized to do so for each party.

Appendix B:
Building the Evaluation Criteria _____

The unique nature of institutions and the ever-changing environment in which they operate make it impossible to develop a timeless set of evaluation criteria that are applicable to all functions on all campuses. However, there is a standard set of questions that an institution should ask itself to facilitate the development of appropriate criteria that can be used to evaluate each operating alternative. Like the decision process itself, these questions can be grouped around the major areas of impact that the contract management/self-operation decision is likely to have. These include:

- Financial

- Human Resources

- Mission & Culture

- Management Control & Efficiency

- Service Quality

- Legal & Ethical Considerations.

The questions that appear below are discussed in greater detail throughout this document. They have been consolidated here to facilitate their use in the project team's discussions.

Financial

- What is the level of investment that the functional area will require from the institution in order to maintain or enhance its operations?

- What is the cost of providing central administrative support services (accounting, human resource, procurement, payroll) to the function?

- How much revenue has the institution forgone by utilizing a contractor? Conversely, what levels and types of costs has the institution not had to bear as the result of contract management?

- Are the revenue and expenses of the functional area in line with those of its peers?

Human Resources

- What is the projected growth in employee compensation, including benefits, likely to be?

- Do employees have the right skills to perform the jobs that are required of them?

- Are employees receiving adequate training?

- Is the workforce unionized?

Mission & Culture

- What are the institution's expectations for the functional area's performance (financial, scope and quality of services, cost to customers)?

- How would employees from other functional areas react to the introduction of a contractor or conversely to a switch to self-operation?

- Do alumni come in contact with this function? What are their expectations for how it would operate?

- What role does the functional area play in supporting the institution's mission and strategy?

Management Control & Efficiency

- Do the policies and procedures of the functional area strike the optimum balance between efficiency and control?

- Are the financial area's operations consistent with industry standards?

- Is management responsive, efficient, and effective?

- Does management work within the fiscal boundaries provided to them?

- Is the functional area's plant and equipment sufficient or is it hindering its ability to provide high-quality service, minimize costs and maximize revenue?

- Does the functional area have the necessary information systems to operate efficiently?

- What level of control does the institution need to retain over the functional area?

Service Quality

- Who are the functional area's customers?

- What types of services do customers expect the functional area to provide?

- Are the needs of customers being met?

- Is the appropriate emphasis being placed on customer satisfaction and quality?

Legal & Ethical Considerations

- What are the potential risks to the institution in operating this functional area?

- Are the functional area's risk management costs in line with those of other functions on campus?

- Does the institution have a need to insulate itself from all or part of the risk associated with this functional area?

- What is the current tax status of the functional area? Is the institution seeking to reduce its exposure to UBIT or property taxes?

- What impact does this function have on the local business community? Is the institution subject to allegations of unfair competition?

- Who maintains responsibility for compliance with local, state, and federal regulations?

By answering these and other questions, the project team will begin to gain an understanding of the issues that are part of the contract management/self-operation decision and the relative importance of each issue in selecting an operating model.

Appendix C:
Directory of Higher Education
Management Associations _____

Association of Collegiate Licensing Administrators (ACLA)

Elizabeth Kennedy, President
University of Southern California
PSX 102
Los Angeles, CA 90089–1333

Association of College and University Housing Officers-International (ACUHO-I)

Gary Schwarzmueller, Executive Director
ACUHO-I Central Office
101 Curl Drive, Suite 140
Columbus, OH 43210–1195

Association of College and University Telecommunications Administrators (ACUTA)

Del Combs, Executive Director
Financial Center, Suite 2420
Lexington, KY 40507

Association of Higher Education Facilities Officers (APPA)

Walter A. Schaw, Executive Vice President
1446 Duke Street
Alexandria, VA 22314–3492

Canadian Association of University Business Officers (CAUBO)

Kenneth Clements, Executive Director
151 Slater
Ottawa, Ontario
Canada K1P 5N1

CAUSE

Jane N. Ryland, President
4840 Pearl East Circle
Suite 302-E
Boulder, CO 80301

College and University Personnel Association (CUPA)

Richard C. Creal, Executive Director
1233 20th Street, NW
Suite 301
Washington, DC 20036

EDUCOM

Steven W. Gilbert, Vice President
1112 16th Street, NW
Washington, DC 20036

National Association of College Auxiliary Services (NACAS)

Stan Clark, Executive Director
P.O. Box 870
Staunton, VA 24401

National Association of College Stores (NACS)

Garis Distelhorst, CAE, Executive Director
500 East Lorain Street
Oberlin, OH 44074

National Association of College and University Business Officers (NACUBO)

Caspa L. Harris Jr., President
One Dupont Circle, NW
Suite 500
Washington, DC 20036

National Association of College & University Food Services (NACUFS)

Joseph H. Spina, Executive Director
1405 South Harrison Road
Suite 303
Manly Miles Building, M.S.U.
East Lansing, MI 48824

National Association of Educational Buyers, Inc. (NAEB)

Neil D. Markee, Executive Vice President
450 Wireless Boulevard
Hauppauge, NY 11788

Society for College and University Planning (SCUP)

Mary Ann Armour, Director
610 E. University
2026M School of Education Building
University of Michigan
Ann Arbor, MI 48109–1259